RUM GULLY TALES *from* TUCK'EM INN

RUM GULLY TALES
from
TUCK'EM INN

Stories of Murrells Inlet and The Waccamaw Country

by Pratt Gasque

SANDLAPPER PUBLISHING, INC.
Orangeburg, South Carolina

Manufactured in the United States of America.

First edition, first printing, 1990.

Book design by Messagemakers
Virginia Ingram and Jane Kelly

Library of Congress Cataloging-in-Publication Data

Gasque, B. Pratt, 1908-
Rum Gully tales from Tuck'em Inn : stories of Murrells Inlet and the Waccamaw country / by B. Pratt Gasque.
p. cm.
Summary: An octogenarian records life and history in and around Murrells Inlet and the Waccamaw country of South Carolina.
ISBN 0-87844-094-1. — ISBN 0-87844-095-X (pbk.)
1. Murrells Inlet Region (S.C.)—History—Juvenile literature. 2. Waccamaw River Region (N.C. and S.C.)—History—Juvenile literature. [1. Murrells Inlet Region (S.C.)—History. 2. Waccamaw River Region (N.C. and S.C.)—History.] I. Title.
F279.M87G37 1990
975.7'87—dc20 89-29438
CIP
AC

ith love and affection this book is dedicated to the Suzannes who have inspired the writer and have contributed so much to his life:

Suzanne (Susan) Arnette Lucas
Suzanne Lucas Gasque
Suzanne Gasque McIntyre
Suzanne Lucas Gasque McIntyre
Suzanne Pratt Regen
Charlotte Suzanne Schneider
Suzanne (Susannah) Small
Suzie Q (a sixteen-foot sloop)
Suzanne (a twenty-seven-foot Barbour Cabin cruiser)
Suzanne II (a twenty-six-foot Richardson Sport cruiser)
Suzanne III (a thirty-three-foot Ulrichsen cruiser)

And with apologies to the *Bachelor*
(a twenty-six-foot Elco raised-deck cruiser)

Contents

Prologue

These are the stories that my father Pratt Gasque would tell us on summer evenings on the porch of Tuck'em Inn, our family cottage at Murrells Inlet. These were the days before television, movie theaters, and local night spots. Story time was our favorite nightly entertainment. The more we heard the tales, the more popular they became. Everyone had a favorite story—mine was the rescue of the fisherman off the shore of Floral Beach (now Surfside) on a freezing December night.

I am most grateful to my father for putting these wonderful *Rum Gully Tales* into print. I feel that it is very important for future generations who will love and enjoy Murrells Inlet.

Suzanne Gasque McIntyre

Acknowledgements

The writer wishes to thank the following persons who helped and encouraged him in writing this book: Mrs. Trudy Bazeman of the Georgetown County Memorial Library, Georgetown, South Carolina; Clarke Willcox, Jr., of the Hermitage, Murrells Inlet; Mrs. Genevieve Chandler Peterkin of Murrells Inlet; Mrs. Eugenia Buck Cutts of Conway and the Inlet and Mrs. Peggy Richardson Hall of Marion for assistance with tales of the Buck family; Mrs. Henry Burroughs, Sr., the late Mr. Burroughs, and Henry, Jr., for help with early churches on the Inlet and stories of their family and the railroad and steamship lines; Tommy Chandler of Murrells Inlet for refreshing my memory of creek names at the Inlet and the lore of the crabbing industry; Mrs. Caroline Berry of the Litchfield Book Shop for her interest and contact with the publisher; Mrs. Alberta Lachicotte Quattlebaum of Waverly plantation for the story of the Lachicotte family and her picture of Waverly Mills; Mrs. Dorothy Chappel of Murrells Inlet for early pictures of the Inlet; Ben Burroughs of Conway for pictures and for allowing the writer to use pictures and stories from the *Horry Historical Society Quarterly;* The Honorable John Patrick Doyle of Georgetown for the picture of the barque, *Henry Buck;* Ray Govus of Marion for his watercolor of Tuck'em Inn; the ladies in the Marion Public Library who so kindly helped with photocopying; Mrs. Robert McIntyre of Marion and Wahee and Miss Angie Groves of Myrtle Beach for typing; and my son B. Pratt Gasque, Jr., for the use of his office and equipment and for his encouragement.

A thousand thanks to my daughter Suzanne Gasque McIntyre and my wife Suzanne who faithfully and patiently listened to my stories and helped with the arrangement of chapters and pictures.

Introduction

Rum Gully Tales do not relate textbook history or trace genealogy of families living at Murrells Inlet or Waccamaw Neck. They are stories I heard as a boy on the porch at Tuck'em Inn or in the servant's quarters playing skin or casino with the creek boys while waiting for the right tide and moon to go striking. Others I heard in the coast guard during World War II or in the navy while battling the North Atlantic on submarine patrol. Many of the stories were told around a campfire on some island or beach or handed down from generation to generation—most of them are true or have some reliable background, and a few are enlarged by the telling and stretched a little by the environment.

As a boy I knew every person at Murrells Inlet, fished and hunted with them, sailed and rowed their boats, and joined them for meals when asked. The Inlet was a grand and fascinating place in which to grow up, with too few hours in the day to do all the inviting things there. Now, as an older person, there is still more to learn about the tides, the currents, and the creatures who live and die in the creeks and marshes.

The joy of sailing a good boat, the thrill of landing a big fish on light tackle, and the excitement of being in a duck blind in the marsh at daybreak whet a boy's curiosity about nature and teach him to cope with life to come.

Pratt Gasque

1

TUCK'EM INN IS BORN

Our family began going to Murrells Inlet in the summer of 1914 when my father John Gasque purchased a lot from Colonel J. Monroe Johnson in the Sunnyside section of Murrells Inlet on Rum Gully Swash.

World War I had begun in Europe, international trade was dead, and business at a standstill. My father was a merchant who operated a department store on Main Street in Marion, South Carolina, where B. C. Moore's store is now located. Business was so bad he was selling almost nothing, and in order to build the house at the Inlet, he traded merchandise from the store for lumber, brick, and other construction materials.

Arthur Evans, a Marion carpenter, and Buck Davis, a local brick mason, were engaged to go to the Inlet and build the house. Plans for the cottage were drawn by my mother Kathryn Pratt Gasque, better known to her children and friends as Muz.

The plan was a camp-style cottage with three bedrooms and an open, but screened, combination dining and living room with a kitchen in back. There was a bathroom with a tub and water piped from an artesian well and an outside shower, but no hot water. If a hot bath was wanted, water was heated on the kitchen stove and carried to the tub. Two servants' rooms and a bath were at the back of the lot.

There was no electricity, and our lights were kerosene angle lamps; a double one hung over the dining room table. It was the children's job each morning before crabbing or swimming to clean the shades and fill the container with oil.

All the materials for the house had to be sent to Conway by train and then loaded on a river boat which made regular runs between Conway and Georgetown. The boat unloaded at Wachesaw Landing, and supplies were brought over to the cottage by ox cart driven by one of the Keith boys, Andrew or George.

The first trip I remember was in the spring of 1914 while the house was being built. Arthur Evans had hired some local helpers, among them the Reverend Catoe Singleton. Besides preaching on Sunday and carpentering during the week, he could play a tune with his hammer, and the other builders worked in time to some familiar tune he tapped out. Catoe was a forebear of the large family of Singletons living at present in and around the Inlet.

The cottage was finished by June 1, 1914, and we prepared to move down for the summer. On the day of departure everyone was up at daybreak. A rack on top of the car was packed with boxes of clothes, curtains, bedding, and housewares, and a crate of live chickens was tied to the running board.

We were underway by eight o'clock as it was an all-day trip. Our Model T Ford touring car was full to overflowing with my father driving and Mother and me in the front seat. Auntie Fan and Kakie, my aunt and cousin, were on the back seat with our two servants, Sipeo and Catherine Sparkman. One of them held my younger brother Jack, who was only eighteen months old.

There were no paved roads and the first adventure was maneuvering a causeway in the swamp and a wooden bridge at Galivants Ferry. There was a stop at Holliday's store to put water in the radiator, let Jack go to the rest room, and check the tires. The road then went by Aynor and on to Cool Spring where we stopped to get fresh eggs from a

Tuck'em Inn, 1914.

Mr. Cooper. The eggs were stored in a bucket under the seat in hopes they would survive the journey.

The Model T had a cloth top and no sides. When it rained, we stopped and put up side curtains which were stored under the seat. From Galivants Ferry to Cool Spring was by far the rainiest area in the country, and the side curtains were brought out several times.

We reached Homewood, about four miles north of Conway, around noon and ate a picnic lunch in a churchyard across from a good artesian well. The well had such a strong flow that it would knock a glass or container out of your hand if you didn't hold it tight, and you would always get a little wet from the splash.

We proceeded through Conway with the horn blowing to scare the dogs and chickens out of the way, then we had to stop for a train. In those days the railroad tracks went down the middle of the main street leaving no room to pass, so we just waited for the train to move on. To pass the time, Dad would visit Barretts Hardware and Muz would stop at Hawes Grocery for some Meadow Gold butter.

After checking tires and putting water in the radiator, we departed Conway on the road to Georgetown. There was

The train to Myrtle Beach ran down Main Street of Conway.

no bridge over the Waccamaw River and the only crossing was at Peachtree Ferry. We left the Georgetown road near Toddville and followed the river road by Bucksville to the ferry. The ferry was operated by a farmer by the name of Rufus Graham who lived on the east side of the river. Usually he was plowing a field on his farm. We would beat a piece of iron on a plowshare hanging from a tree, and Rufus would take his mules to the barn, unhitch them, and put them in their stalls. Then he would amble down to the ferry which was a flat boat only large enough for one automobile. After checking his cables and nodding a greeting to us, he pulled the ferry to our side of the Waccamaw.

The ferry was pulled with wooden mauls about the size of a baseball bat. Grooves in the large end were placed on the cable, and the flat was moved by hand. When he reached our side of the river, he secured the flat to a tree with a stout cable which kept the automobile from pushing the flat away from the bank when it was driven on board. The car wheels were carefully chocked, the cable was loosened, and we would cross the river. On reaching the other side the same procedure was repeated, and the automobile was driven off.

The Peachtree Ferry, circa 1914, near Socastee, was the only way to cross the Waccamaw River en route to Murrells Inlet or Myrtle Beach.

After paying the toll of fifty cents, we traveled a dirt and corduroy road to Socastee, where we made a stop at Cooper's store to rest after the river crossing, to buy vegetables, and check the tires and radiator.

There was another long wooden bridge across Socastee Creek, then we felt that we were on the home stretch with all the rivers behind us and nothing but sand and mud ahead.

After a couple of stops to check the tires and let the radiator cool from traveling in low gear through the sand, we reached Burgess where we stopped at Marlowe's store to find out if the bridge was passable over Collins Creek and to reserve some chickens for the next week.

Murrells Inlet from the front porch at Tuck'em Inn.

There was always a lengthy discussion from front to back seat as to whether the tide would be in or out and whether there would be time for a swim before supper.

We finally arrived at Tuck'em Inn while the tide was high. The car was unpacked, the house unlocked, and the shutters unbolted. We were ready to settle in for the summer.

2

EARLY DAYS AT THE INLET

For years there has been controversy about the Inlet's name, whether it should be Murrells, Murrel, or Morrall's Inlet. There was even a movement to change the spelling after Dr. George C. Rogers, Jr., in his history of Georgetown County stated that the name came from a John Morrall who purchased 631 acres of land on and around the Inlet in 1731 from Anthony Matthews.

In 1756 the Royal Governor of South Carolina appointed a commission to build a road from Waccamaw Ferry near Georgetown following the coast through Waccamaw Neck to the Cape Fear River. Called the King's Road, it was first to open the Inlet to land travel. The Gaillard-Cook map of South Carolina in 1770 shows the Inlet with no name but with a family named Murrel living nearby.

The Henry Mouzon map of 1770 of North and South Carolina names the Inlet Murrel and shows a family by the same name living there. The first United States census taken in 1790 lists a John Morrall living in All Saints Parish with eight children and sixty slaves. In 1800 the census shows a William Murrell living in Winyah County, South Carolina, but no Morralls. On Mills' Atlas of 1825 the Inlet is called Murray's Inlet, and nearby families are Belin, Weston, Allston, and Withers.

In rummaging through old manuscripts and looking at old charts and maps of the South Carolina coast, I found interesting things about the Inlet. The processing and shipping of salt was the first and most important industry there, as salt was a necessary and sometimes scarce commodity in the seventeenth and eighteenth centuries. It was needed for the preservation of foods such as pork and other meats and for packing fish, for tanning hides to make saddles and other leather goods, and for medicine. During the Revolutionary War many a bushel of salt was made and distributed to our troops and people from this area.

Mills' Atlas of 1825 shows two salt works on the Inlet, and there were many more mobile units brought in from time to time. In summer large, shallow iron pans or vats filled with sea water were exposed to the sun to evaporate the liquid and leave salt. In winter and at other times they would build fires under the vats to hasten the evaporation. After the water was evaporated, they would scrape the salt from the vats and pack it in bags or boxes. Portable salt pans were brought near the water by horse and wagon, then a bucket brigade was formed by slaves or other help to fill them with sea water.

This type of salt making was used up to and after the War Between the States, when Northern ships came up the Waccamaw River, burned and pillaged some of the plantation houses, and raided the salt works at Murrells Inlet. The Confederates ran blockade runners into the Inlet, and their cargoes were unloaded on the Inlet side, carried by wagons across Waccamaw Neck, and reloaded on smaller boats to be taken where needed.

The timbers of one of these blockade runners have recently been uncovered on the beach near Debordieu and the story is that another blockade runner was driven ashore and burned on Magnolia Beach which is now the upper end of Huntington State Park, near where the old mouth of the Inlet was located.

Around 1880 the Burroughs Collins Company of Conway established a steamship line on the Waccamaw River to make runs from Georgetown to Conway three times a week.

Mrs. Flossie Sarvis Morris, who lives near the Waccamaw, with the salt pan her grandfather used for salt making before the Civil War.

They stopped at landings along the way and carried passengers bound for Murrells Inlet or Pawleys Island. Mail bound for the Inlet was left at the Laurel Hill Landing, named for an old plantation, and taken to the Inlet by horse or ox cart. The local post office, also called Laurel, started in the old Belin Methodist Church parsonage, and Samuel S. Dusenbury was appointed postmaster in 1890.

If one wanted to go to the Inlet or another section of Waccamaw Neck from the inland, one traveled to Conway or Georgetown by train, spent the night in a hotel, and caught an early steamboat to the landing on the river nearest his destination. A horse and buggy or ox cart had to be engaged to complete the trip.

The Keith Express, owned and operated by Andrew and George Keith, met steamboats at Wachesaw Landing and delivered freight and supplies to residents of Murrells Inlet.

Some of the boats had sleeping accommodations and served meals and enjoyed a reputation for good food. A number of the notable cooks at the Inlet and Pawleys Island learned their trade on the boats. The story goes that the proprietor of Oliver's Lodge at the Inlet was captain on one of the river boats and took some of the help with him when he opened his inn and restaurant.

A yoke of oxen and a sturdy wagon were available as Inlet transportation courtesy of George and Andrew Keith. They carried passengers to their destinations and hauled the freight and supplies, including ice, from the boat landing at Wachesaw to the Inlet.

The first bridge across the river was built about 1919 at Conway near the old Quattlebaum ice plant, and the steamboats and ox carts gradually gave way to autos and trucks. I vividly remember the first ice received at Tuck'em Inn by truck from the Quattlebaum Ice Company. We could buy as little as fifty pounds instead of the three-hundred-pound block which formerly came by steamboat.

An almost forgotten industry at Murrells Inlet was the catching and raising of diamondback terrapins for market.

The first bridge across the Waccamaw River at Conway, circa *1919.*

Terrapin soup was quite a delicacy in the fine hotels of New York, Boston, and Baltimore around the turn of the century, and they would purchase all they could obtain. The diamondback terrapin is a saltwater variety of the freshwater terrapins and is so named for the diamondlike markings on its back. These turtles are found mostly in the coastal waters of the southeastern United States and Gulf of Mexico.

I have seen these turtles being raised only once when I was a small boy. The owner of the turtle farm, a Mr. Barbee of Isle of Hope near Savannah, Georgia, had one pet turtle named Toby. He had trained it to pick up its right front foot when he said "how do you do."

The diamondback terrapins were so in demand that they became almost extinct about 1915, and a law was passed forbidding their capture or sale. The terrapins are coming back now, and we are catching some of them in the crab traps. Maybe Inlet restaurants will soon be serving terrapin soup.

In 1914 the Inlet's permanent residents were fishermen, farmers, boat captains, small merchants, a couple of blacksmiths, and a few derelicts who had come there to fish and just stayed on.

Captains Morse and Leonard took out fishing parties in open Seabright skiffs about twenty feet long, powered with one-cylinder Lathrop engines which would run all day on a gallon of gas. To fish from daybreak to dark cost five dollars a person or twenty dollars for the boat, and the fishing was good.

A Captain Dozier farmed what is now Wagon Wheel Farms, and the story was that Mrs. Dozier, a member of a prominent Columbia family, ran away to marry the captain and raise her delightful family. When I was about twelve years old, Mrs. Dozier would let me shoot squirrels in the woods behind her house.

The Gilmore Smiths had bought Sunnyside, the pre-Civil War house built as a summer home by rice planter J. Motte Alston. They lived in the house and farmed the surrounding property with their children Nan, Luther, Ashby, and Mary, who is now Mrs. Walker and still lives in the house.

The Brown family ran a store on the road from the present day drugstore to Wachesaw Landing. The first post office I remember was at this store. Douglas Brown, appointed postmaster in 1919, was the grandfather of Brownie of the Inlet nursery and yard service and Buddy, who worked with Wayne Gordon at the Gulf station and later for Brookgreen Gardens.

The Dal Johnsons with their daughter Mittie lived at Vaux Hall, and nearby were the Sam Stevensons with their son Wilbur. Vaux Hall was an old summer cottage originally owned by the Vaux family who lived and planted rice on Sandy Island.

Mrs. Dal Johnson was named postmistress in 1913 when the office name was changed from Laurel to Murrells Inlet, and she relocated it in Vaux Hall. The post office had been in Vaux Hall from 1898 to 1911 under Postmistress Ida Beaty. Her successor James S. Vick had moved it and run it from his house on the old road to Pawleys Island.

Other plantations were occupied by the Clarke Willcox family, who had purchased the plantation at Wachesaw

A swimming party at Curlew Point, 1915. From left to right, Kathryn P. Gasque, my mother; Mary Munsell, Bessie B. Gasque, and, in the water, Pratt Gasque with his uncle, Joseph H. Gasque, holding my younger brother Jack.

Landing and were permanent residents at the Hermitage, the creek house of their plantation. The Henry Willcox family lived at Woodland, one of the first summer cottages of the rice planters built by the Nesbits whose plantation was on Black River.

The Fred Grants and their son Happy lived on the creek near the Methodist parsonage. Mr. Grant was magistrate. The first Methodist minister I remember in the parsonage was the Reverend Scoggins, who had several boys.

The Joe Vereens and the Bossy Vereens were on the Socastee Road just beyond the Tom Lees, and Gordon Vereen ran a store near the present entrance to Mt. Gilead. The Mitchell Watts lived on the corner where the old road to Conway meets Highway 17.

There was a family of Carsons who owned all the land

from Mt. Gilead to Rum Gully Swash and about a mile inland. Their first house washed away in the hurricane of 1893, so John F. Carson went a mile inland and built another. He ran a store on a country road near the house of Jim Heyward. When the traffic by Mr. Carson's store and house exceeded five cars a day, he dug a small ditch across the road at each end of his property. If you didn't slow to under five miles an hour, you would surely break a spring or be thrown through the top of the car. Mr. Carson was an uncle of the Jordan brothers and, I believe, left them the property they now own at Jordan's Landing. Once my mother sent me to Carson's store for syrup, and I took a pail to bring it home in. When Mr. Carson failed to fill the pail to the top, I called it to his attention, knowing that my mother liked good measure and would scold me for spilling the syrup on the way home. Mr. Carson said the pail would be full when I reached home, and he was right. The syrup foamed and bubbled to the top of the pail as I walked and was running over when I reached the cottage.

Near the entrance to Mt. Gilead there was a blacksmith's shop owned by Derick Jordan. He was an uncle of Tommy Jordan who was postmaster at the Inlet from 1949 to 1977.

One of the most interesting families at the Inlet was the Howard Wesleys. Mr. Wesley had a museum in the living room of his house which was located on an old road to Pawleys Island. A good storyteller, he claimed that he was the son of an English nobleman who ran away from home after a dispute with his father and came to America, first to Virginia and then to Murrells Inlet. When we had guests, my father always took them to meet Mr. Wesley and see the museum. The Wesleys had a son Howard and several daughters.

Another family I remember at the Inlet were the Stricklands and their son Charlie. The Turbevilles lived near the Socastee Road and always had good sweet potatoes for sale. Mr. Van Turbeville dried them in the second story of a barn, and that seemed to make them better.

Alex Sing was an expert driller of artesian wells. When he dug our well using mules to turn the bit, it was quite a sight to see the two mules walking in circles and driving the bit down to water. Mr. Sing was the father of Alex and Tommy, who both operated charter boats.

The Eason family came to the Inlet about 1917 with, I believe, Eddie coming first and opening a small store. His father came later, and they bought property where the Back Porch Restaurant is now and opened a store near the one Danny Eason now operates. The Easons were a colorful family, and my father always enjoyed swapping cigars with Mr. Eason and discussing business. They were very accommodating and always assured you that anything you needed and they were out of would surely arrive with the afternoon mail.

The Nance family came to the Inlet about the same time as the Easons. He was a commercial fisherman and his son Paul opened a restaurant. The family is now prominent in all phases of the seafood export business, operating a restaurant and shipping wholesale to eastern markets.

I also remember my good friends the Hewitts, father and mother of Levi, and the Wilson family. The Wilsons lived near Wachesaw on River Road and operated a sawmill. Herman Wilson lived in Marion for several years, then moved back to the Inlet and became magistrate.

The summer colony at the Inlet before World War I consisted of about thirty cottages on the waterfront in a small area between Rum Gully Swash on the north and Woodland on the south.

There were four distinct little settlements with the largest being Sunnyside, named for the old J. Motte Alston house. As mentioned earlier, the house is owned by the Gilmore Smiths.

Walking north from the Smith house, the first summer cottage was owned by the O.H. Foley family from Sumter; next were the R.J. Blackwells from Marion, Dr. Julius Mood from Sumter, the E.T. Willcox and Howard Cross families

The summer home of Julia Peterkin at Murrells Inlet.

from Marion, the William Peterkins from Fort Motte, the Henry Bucks, the Henry Mullinses, the J.D. Murchisons, the E.T. Hugheses, the W.K. Davis family, and the John Gasques, all from Marion.

Dr. Julius Mood was the father of Mrs. William (Julia) Peterkin whose cottage was three doors down. Here and on Brookgreen plantation she gathered material about slaves in the plantation country. Her book, *Scarlet Sister Mary*, remains the only work of literature by a South Carolinian to win a Pulitzer Prize. Pretend, the Peterkin cottage, and Tuck'em Inn are the only cottages in the Sunnyside section now occupied by the same families as in 1914.

South of the Sunnyside house was the cottage of the Sam Norwoods of Marion. Lou Norwood Haskell tells me that it was built in 1914, the same year we built Tuck'em Inn. There is a story that the Norwood girls had a house party soon after the house was completed. Among the guests was a girl from Serbia, a student at Converse College with Elizabeth and Lou. Some of the boys at the party slipped sand fiddlers in the girls' beds. When the Serbian girl saw

The Hermitage, 1845, summer home of the Flagg family of Wachesaw plantation and now the residence of Clarke Willcox, Jr.

the fiddlers, she called, "Meeses Norwood, Meeses Norwood, I see bugs, I think I faint." And indeed she did. Blamed for this prank were the late Dick Willcox and William Hubbard.

Soon after the Norwood cottage was finished, William and L.L. Pettigrew built a house next door. The Hunter family built south of the Pettigrews several years later.

There were no cottages between the Hermitage and the Methodist parsonage at this time, but the McKoy Roses built in the area soon after World War I. This section of the Inlet was called the Hermitage.

In the area around the parsonage, there was, besides that building and Oliver's Lodge, a cottage occupied by the Walter Stackhouse family including Mrs. Stackhouse's brother Dr. Waller, who was a professor at Wofford College. Living south of Oliver's Lodge were the Kings from Aynor with their children Capitola, Mary Winnefred, and William, who still spends his summers in the King cottage, another house being used by the second generation.

The A.C. Jones family from Batesburg was next. There were no houses between them and the Grants, as the Foxworth and Byars families did not build until after the war. The Grants lived in the last house in the Parsonage section of the Inlet.

After leaving the Grants and crossing a footbridge across the swash, you reached the fourth section where an open field next to the Sam Stevensons and then vacant lots led to Vaux Hall. The old Buck house stood at Bucks Landing, but it was unoccupied and in a bad state of repair. The Beaty family from Georgetown owned and occupied a cottage between the Buck house and Woodland, owned by the Henry Willcox family in 1914 and later sold to Taylor Baker of Marion.

This was the entire summer colony when I was a small boy. I knew all of the owners and I usually knew if they had guests, because I walked from Tuck'em Inn to the post office almost every day and brought back any mail for anyone along the waterfront. For this service, I often got a cookie or a piece of cake, but, more important, I always knew if there was a pretty girl visiting on the Inlet or if someone had a new boat.

The old post office at Murrells Inlet, circa 1921.

3

THE TIDES

Many afternoons and nights on the porch at Tuck'em Inn, the conversation dwelt on the tides, their rise and fall and what caused them. Children visiting for the first time could be told that there was a big stopper in the mouth of the Inlet and if you pulled it out, the water would leave and it would be low tide. With the stopper in, the Inlet filled up and made high tide.

As we grew and learned a little more about the tides and ocean currents, we found that we always had a really high tide at full moon and lower than normal on the opposite moon phase. Then we learned there are fifty-two influences on the tide.

Soon after graduating from Clemson, my brother Jack was employed by the United States Coast and Geodetic Survey in Washington to operate the machine that provided tidal data. They would factor in fifty-two different conditions which controlled the tides. The moon had the strongest pull, the sun next the strongest, and so on with all the planets and major stars having their influence. If all of these factors were pulling against each other, we had very low tides called neap.

Then there was the question of why the difference between the high and low tide in some areas was much greater than in others. Murrells Inlet has a rise and fall of between five and six feet. Charleston has about seven feet, but at

Thunderbolt near Savannah, the rise and fall reaches twelve feet. Farther south at Brunswick, Georgia, the difference is near fifteen feet. Then it diminishes, and on reaching the Indian River in Florida, there is only a foot of tide. These differences are caused by the different shapes and depths of the bays and sounds and the type of land mass under the waters.

Some years ago I visited the Bay of Fundy off the coast of New Brunswick Province in Canada. The rise and fall of tides there is an amazing fifty feet, and it comes in so fast and furious that those who work on boats in those waters never try to buck the flow but make it work for them. Near Moncton, New Brunswick, the tide comes up the Petitcodiac River with a three-foot wave. They call this a tidal bore. Several other places in the world have this phenomenal tidal wave, and it is awesome to watch. At a rocky place on this river they have what they call "reversing falls," because the tide rushing in looks like a waterfall in one direction and when it starts out looks like falls in the opposite direction.

The tides and ocean currents are an interesting subject and some people make this study their life's work. Sailors and ships' captains have used their knowledge of the winds and tides for several hundred years.

When the Spaniards owned countries in South America and some of the islands in the Caribbean such as Puerto Rico and Cuba, they would load their treasure ships, and follow the prevailing winds easterly until they reached the Gulf Stream. Then they would ride the Gulf Stream north about two thirds of the way up the Florida coast, where the prevailing winds changed to westerlies. Turning on these westerlies, they sailed back to Spain. This is the reason there were so many Spanish ships wrecked off the Florida Keys while they were beating up the coast of Florida on their way home.

The rise and fall of the tides from the porch at Tuck'em Inn create different panoramas according to whether the tide is high, low, or in between. The skilled creek boys who worked along the Inlet had a tidal language of their own such as flood tide when the tide was coming in, young flood when the tide had just turned in, ebb when the tide was going out, and slack tide when it was at dead high or dead low. There is a short cut through Little and Big Whale creeks called "no man's friend," for no matter what the phase of tide, there is always a part in which you have to row against the flow.

Now the scientists and oceanographers say that the factors that influence the tides only pull on the water, but I have a theory that the factors also pull on the land masses under the water. If you talk to an old gravedigger or ditchdigger, he will tell you that when digging a hole during some phases of the moon you will have more dirt left over than you need and at other phases you will not have enough left to fill the hole or grave. This is not a tall tale or fantasy, but a theory researched and proved by the Rum Gully Oceanographic Foundation!

4

INLET SEAFOOD

Murrells Inlet is called the seafood capital of the Grand Strand. Inlet seafood has become so famous that those who catch it don't have to ship it away, for people will drive hundreds of miles to order it prepared to their taste at one of our fine restaurants or purchase it at a local market to freeze and take home.

When the last clam season opened on September 15, more than a hundred boats in the Inlet gathered clams for local restaurants and for shipping to northern dealers. In addition to clam gatherers, many more were gathering oysters, fish, and crabs.

For a long time Oliver's Lodge was the only place that served meals at the Inlet, and the person who was responsible for those good meals was Tina Vereen, the wife of Mac Oliver. The Vereen family has been associated with good cooking and good food in and near the Inlet for several generations. It was no accident that George Washington picked a good cook when he made his southern tour after the Revolutionary War and spent a night near Little River at the home of Jeremiah Vereen.

Back in the plantation days, the planter would choose from his slaves one boy who was good at fishing and hunting and who could find the best oysters and shrimp; who was a good shot and could bring in deer, duck, marsh hens, and rice birds and prepare them for the cook. Called creek

Oliver's Lodge, the first boarding house and restaurant at the Inlet.

boys, they also prepared the oak fires for oyster roasts and took the roasted oysters from the fire and dropped them in saucers of hot butter for the guests.

These early oyster roasts were usually held outdoors on the front lawn or in the garden. The oysters were washed and stacked in a horseshoe shape with their mouths to the fire of carefully selected oak which was laid inside in the horseshoe. Clams were also served, but not as in New England clambakes. Usually they were opened and cooked on the half shell in an outdoor oven with a piece of salt pork or bacon the size of a penny on top. When the meat curled a little or sizzled, they were served to eager guests.

Before World War I families at the Inlet still employed boys or men to catch and prepare seafood for the cook and to take members of the household to the best fishing spots. Creek boys usually became cooks or held down both jobs. At Tuck'em Inn, we hired Sam Goeback and Richard Knox and, later, Sipeo Sparkman. Sip stayed with the family for sixty-three years both at the Inlet and in Marion. He also cooked for the White Oak Fishing Club on the Pee Dee River to which my father belonged.

James Heyward, one of the best fishermen and cooks at the Inlet died in 1985. At the age of eighty-two he could still put a meal fit for a king on the table. Another of the greats, George Singleton, died in 1987 at the age of ninety.

These men were my good friends, and I learned much from them as a boy. They showed me the best fishing spots, where and when to haul for shrimp, how to set a net to rob a creek, and how to keep my hands out of stone crab holes.

We fished with hand lines using shrimp for bait, and it wasn't unusual to bring in forty or fifty fish in an hour or two of fishing. The usual catch consisted of trout, whiting,

Jim Heyward, one of the Inlet's famous cooks, serving steamed clams at a party at Tuck'em Inn in the fall of 1978.

Buster Allston opening clams for a party at the Inlet, circa 1965.

croaker, and yellowtail, with a bass or two in spring and fall.

Creek boys taught me how to play skin, black jack, stealing casino, and sometimes we rolled dice while waiting for the tide and moon to be right for striking. Striking was gigging flounder at night with a light made by a lightwood fire built in a wire rack and suspended over the side of a flat-bottomed boat. A person with a gig would be in the front and the back of the boat, and as it was poled through shallow water they would try to spear the flounder buried in the sand. It was a satisfying way to catch fish, but it was usually an all-night affair. You came home smelling of tar, turpentine, and woodsmoke.

They also taught me to bog for crabs in mud flats. We could catch a bucketful in an hour or so. Blue channel crabs were the most plentiful variety. Little children and visitors crabbed from a pier with a fish head tied on a string as bait. When the crab fastened on the bait, it could be captured in a dip net.

For a few years around World War II, professional crabbers caught them with a trot line, a long piece of quarter-inch rope baited every three to six feet and anchored at both ends with a buoy for identification. They would have a spool over the side of a rowboat or small inboard and put the line over the spool and dip the crabs as they came over the side. The boat would be propelled by a slow inboard motor or by sculling, and the crabs would be dropped into a half barrel or tub just in front of the crabber. These trot lines were baited with salt eel or ham skins.

The professional crabbers and a lot of residents now use crab traps baited with fish heads or chicken backs. For some strange reason the crabs have developed a taste for chicken. I think this is the result of Billy King's going into the Kentucky Fried Chicken business and feeding the crabs the chickens he doesn't sell.

Crabs, unlike most other animals, grow by shedding their old shells and growing new ones, and that is where we get the soft-shell crabs—between the old and new shells.

The stone crab, which is not as plentiful, has a fat body and large powerful claws. They live in holes in the oyster rocks, and to get them there, you have to reach in and pull them out. This is risky business for they can bite with those powerful claws and have been known to take a finger. Mrs. Genevieve Willcox Chandler was the only woman I've ever heard of who would put her hands in a stone crab hole.

As a boy I spent hours watching fiddler crabs congregate off the sandbars or mud flats. Male sand fiddlers are tan colored and have one large claw they wave to attract females. I used to imagine they were great armies assembling for war and waving their claws to challenge their opponents.

I later read that fiddlers have a built-in tidal rhythm. When some of them were moved from the New Jersey coast to

Off for a picnic on the beach are: left to right, Mr. and Mrs. E.T. Hughes, Sr., with their son E.T. Hughes, Jr., Jack and Pratt Gasque and a friend, and Phyllis and Jim Heyward, circa *1916.*

a research laboratory in the Midwest, they continued to go into their holes and come out based on the time of high and low tide back in New Jersey. Fiddlers make good fishing bait, especially for sheephead.

Since evaporating and selling salt was an important industry on the Inlet before the Revolutionary War, it's not surprising that preserving the bountiful fish harvest with salt soon followed. Packing of fish in salt became an important business and remained so until the coming of the freezing process. Rice planters gave their hands salt fish to replace the salt sweated away in the fields.

In the fall of 1923, I spent several days at one of the fish camps on an island off the Inlet and watched and helped with catching and packing the fish. About twenty-five boys and men in the fishing party camped on the beach. We had one large rowboat or skiff with a long seine carefully folded on the stern. The boat stayed offshore waiting for a school of mullet or spot, then the men on the boat dropped the net around the school of fish and signaled the men and boys on shore to start pulling it in. Sometimes there would be a ton or more of fish, and they were sorted in large tubs or barrels. Benches were set up to begin cleaning and slitting them. After they were washed, they were packed in kegs with salt between each layer. It was an art to know just how much salt to add to keep the fish from spoiling. The kegs of fish were transported to the landing at the Inlet by boat and were sold to wholesale grocers or fish dealers who would in turn sell them to their customers.

Up until World War II, we always had a keg of salt mullet on the back porch, and nothing was better on a winter morning than salt mullet and grits cooked only as a Vereen, Sparkman, or Heyward could cook them.

In the 1930s Eloise and Charlie Edwards built an eating establishment on the west side of Highway 17 known as the Garden City Grill. Not long after, Mr. and Mrs. John Loud opened the Clipper Ship Restaurant across the road. Maybe you have already guessed that these ladies were granddaughters of John Vereen who owned Longwood plantation and entertained George Washington.

Business was picking up for the Murrells Inlet and Garden City eating places, and their reputation for good food was spreading. Pretty soon Lee's Inlet Kitchen was opened by a lady who had worked at the Garden City Grill. Undoubtedly she took along some of those good Vereen recipes. Then, Lucy Vereen Bailey, another granddaughter, and her husband Jim purchased the Wayside Restaurant and improved it with the Vereen touch.

When the Baileys had made all the money they needed, they sold the Wayside to their nephew Sammy Vereen; two other nephews with the advice and help of Aunt Lucy purchased the Sunnyside Restaurant. Those nephews are Bubbie and Johnnie Vereen. Four of the Vereen family restaurants are still operating.

So if you want a good meal at the Inlet and you are not sure which place to try, you just ask if they have a Vereen in the kitchen. When I told this story to Jim Heyward, his reply was that you better believe that when those Vereens are preparing and serving good food, they have a Sparkman or a Heyward in the kitchen doing the seasoning. Perhaps he is right.

5

WACCAMAW COUNTRY

One of the most beautiful rivers in the Eastern United States has its origin in Lake Waccamaw in Columbus County, North Carolina. The name comes from a tribe of Indians, and on some of the old maps it is spelled "Waggama." From the lake, the Waccamaw River winds its way south picking up water from the many swamps and small streams of the lowlands. It enters South Carolina and Horry County near Longs Crossroads then turns westerly to flow past Conway before turning south once more.

Legend has it that the US Corps of Engineers first planned to take the Intracoastal Waterway up the river past Conway and connect it by canal to Little River or Calabash instead of using its present route through Socastee Creek and the canal behind Myrtle Beach. This last section of the waterway was completed about 1936.

The Intracoastal Waterway joins the Waccamaw near Enterprise Landing and Socastee Creek, passes Bucksport, and turns toward the coast behind Murrells Inlet, Litchfield Beach, and Pawleys Island before joining the Black and Pee Dee rivers near Georgetown. Following Winyah Bay south about five miles, the waterway proceeds through the Minim Creek Canal behind South Island, across the two Santee Rivers, and on south. The waterway guidebook describes this teaming with the Waccamaw as one of the prettiest sections on the waterway's entire route from Maine to Florida.

The river has played an important part in the settlement, development, and history of the Waccamaw peninsula for which it defines the western boundary. To the east on the coast lie the great beaches that have come to be known as South Carolina's Grand Strand: Cherry Grove, Myrtle, Surfside, Garden City, Murrells Inlet, Huntington, Litchfield, Pawleys Island, and Debordieu. For Indians who fished, hunted, and traveled on the river and gave it its name and settlers who applied for grants of land along its banks and established forts and townships, the river was food and transportation. Kinston was an early township. It is now Conway.

Long before the white man came to the Waccamaw peninsula, American Indians were coming to fish and gather clams and oysters in Murrells Inlet. If you get in a boat at Sunnyside Landing or the Parsonage and travel Main Creek until you reach Little Whale Creek, then travel on this creek until you are about three hundred yards past where you turn into Big Whale Creek, you will see a small island. On this island the grass grows a little differently, and the marsh is a little greener. You will find a circular mound of shells piled up here by the Indians many, many years ago.

This mound of shells, or shell midden as the archaeologists call it, is where the Indians, possibly four thousand years ago or more, had their feasts and performed their ceremonial dances. The mound is packed by broken clam and oyster shells, and there is a perfect moat around the outside of the ring where canoes or bateaux could be left while the ceremony was going on.

We do not know what tribes of Indians formed this shell midden or what time of the year they put on their act, but we would guess they were Waccamaws, Peedees, Catawbas, and Cheraws and that they picked a pretty time in the spring or fall when the moon was full. We would also guess that they invited other tribes to join them and that each tribe would try to out do the other in their dances and ceremonies. They may even have had a Canadian week and invited tribes such as the Mohicans and the Micmacs.

The Indians were followed by the early European explorers who traded with the Indians and who learned much from them about the art of fishing and gathering shellfish. The explorers were followed by the indigo and rice planters who lived the good life and, with the aid of slaves, sent their crops to faraway markets. After the colonial planters, came commercial fishermen in the eighteen hundreds with their menhaden boats, trawlers, and clammers. They loaded their catches on schooners for northern markets.

In addition to the Waccamaw River's being a means of transportation for settlers in the region, it has other interesting features. One of these is that the Waccamaw and Great Pee Dee rivers flow parallel within a few miles of each other for thirty miles from the border of Horry County to Winyah Bay. Since the Waccamaw has the lower elevation, it takes or drains almost all of the water from the Pee Dee through a number of connecting creeks. Just before reaching Georgetown, the Waccamaw is a large river more than a mile wide, and the Pee Dee has been reduced to a small stream barely one hundred yards across.

The largest of the creeks which transfer the water to the Waccamaw is Bull Creek, draining over one-half of the upper Pee Dee's water. This creek is the boundary between Horry County and Sandy Island in Georgetown County. A regular ferry across Bull Creek once served plantations on Sandy Island.

The island contains around thirty thousand acres of high sandy land with old dunes and alluvial deposits brought down by the two rivers and left when the ocean receded thousands of years ago. It is inhabited by about two hundred black people, and very black they are with no dilution from Indian or white ancestors, but directly descended from rice plantation workers before the War Between the States. Some of them bought their land, some were given their plots by

Sandy Island children enter the only floating school bus in South Carolina.

former owners, and others were squatters who just stayed on the plantation where they had worked.

There are Singletons, Mazycks, Pyatts, Washingtons, Alstons, and Belins, all prominent South Carolina family names that were associated with this area since its settlement in the sixteenth century. They live in three small settlements on the island: Mt. Arena near the boat landing on the Waccamaw side, where most of the people or visitors cross the river; Ruinsville, not far distant inland; and Belin, nearer the Pee Dee River.

The islanders have two churches, Baptist and Methodist, and they once had a school, but now the school-age children are taken across the river on a boat operated and maintained by the state and the county school system. This is the only floating school bus in South Carolina. The boat crosses the river and the children are loaded on regular school buses

Wachesaw Landing on the Waccamaw River, circa *1910.*

and taken to high school in Georgetown or grammar school behind Pawleys Island.

There are no stores on the island, and the inhabitants purchase their supplies on the mainland. A number of them work at Brookgreen or Myrtle Beach and use rowboats or an outboard motor to cross the river. They can leave their automobiles parked at a landing on the mainland just south of Brookgreen.

The next creek south of Bull Creek to connect the two rivers is Thoroughfare, which joins the Pee Dee at Hasty Point and is the southern boundary of Sandy Island. History has it that Hasty Point received its name from a hasty retreat by Francis Marion with a small body of men to escape the Bristish during the Revolutionary War. Thoroughfare Creek has been a popular place for boating and skiing during the last few years and is good for duck hunting and fishing in season.

Other creeks that connect the two rivers are Little Bull, Squirrel, Schooner, and Jericho with a number of smaller ones in between.

A group gathers at Wachesaw Landing at the store owned by Clarke Willcox, Sr., standing in doorway. Among those in the group are Louise Norwood Haskell, Floramay Holliday McLeod, Mrs. C.P. Roberts, and two Serbian girls.

From Collins Creek near Wachesaw plantation the river runs within a mile or two of the Atlantic Ocean for almost twenty-five miles until it enters the ocean between North and South islands at the mouth of Winyah Bay. In all the years that maps have been made of the South Carolina coast, a new inlet to the ocean has never been cut to exhaust the tremendous volume of water built up by hurricanes, rains, and natural drainage.

Hurricanes have been hitting the coast for ages with the worst in 1758, 1822, 1893, 1916, and 1954. All of them did much damage, and one cut a new mouth to Murrells Inlet about a mile north of the old mouth. Between 1893 and Hurricane Hazel in 1954, there were two mouths with an island between. Even the worst of these storms did not cut through to the Waccamaw River.

6

INLET CHURCHES

When we built Tuck'em Inn in 1914 there were no churches at Murrells Inlet. An Episcopalian could attend All Saints on the River Road behind Pawleys Island, and a Methodist could attend Bethel Methodist Church about three miles north of Sunnyside on the old Conway Road. A Baptist would need to go to Collins Creek Baptist Church on the same road about two miles on towards Socastee. A Presbyterian would have to go to Kingston and cross the Waccamaw River at Peachtree Ferry or ferry from Hagley to Georgetown and attend church there. Either would be an all-day journey to get there and back.

Black churchgoers had organized Heaven's Gate Methodist Church in 1872 and Jordan Chapel and Jerusalem Baptist churches before the turn of the century.

Now whether the permanent residents of the Inlet did not attend church or whether they did their worshiping on the beautiful creeks and on the ocean, I can't say, but it was not until after the summer people began coming that the churches began to sprout up.

In 1920 the Methodists, under the urging of Captain Oliver, Mrs. Genevieve Chandler, and the Clarke Willcoxes, decided to build a church on the creek next to Oliver's Lodge on land left to the Methodist Conference by the Reverend James Belin. Named Belin Memorial Methodist Church, the

Residents going to church at Murrells Inlet, circa *1910.*

church attracted most of the members from Bethel. Bethel was discontinued in 1945.

The Presbyterians began a mission called Little Memorial Presbyterian Church in 1925, started by the Kingston Presbyterian Church in Conway under the pastorship of the Reverend J. Mills Lemon. Why the Georgetown church did not sponsor this church I can't say, for the Conway church had to get special permission from the Harmony and Pee Dee presbyteries to colonize out of their territory.

The Baptists seemed to be content with the Collins Creek Baptist Church organized in 1880, which was strong and known as God's Country Church. In 1939 the Baptists organized the Murrells Inlet Baptist Church under the leadership of the Reverend A.D. Woodle, and more than twenty members transferred their memberships from Collins Creek on the opening day. Some of these were Mrs. Luther Smith, Mrs. Ailine Gordon, Mrs. Sam Outlaw, and Mr. and Mrs. Edward Byrd.

In recalling the history of churches in this area, we start with the first church in the Pee Dee section of South

Belin United Methodist Church, built in 1920.

Carolina, established on the Black River about sixteen miles above Georgetown near Brown's Ferry.

The colony of South Carolina was under the parish system controlled by the Church of England. There was not a parish or church east of the Santee River because settlement in this area was jeopardized by threat of Indians. However, some settlers did come into the Black River and Black Mingo area and a few lived on Sampit River. They petitioned the General Assembly for a church, and in 1721 an act was passed establishing a parish east of the Santee. Bounds of this first parish were the Cape Fear River on the north, the Santee River on the south, the Atlantic Ocean on the east, and west as far as His Majesty's subjects might settle. The parish was named Prince George Winyah and a church was built on a beautiful bluff on a horseshoe bend of the Black River. This was the first and only church in the whole Pee Dee section of South Carolina. Reverend Thomas Morritt, the first rector, recorded five hundred Christian whites in his parish.

Soon after, Georgetown was laid out and settled by a Baptist minister named Elisha Screven. In planning the town, he gave lots for a Church of England, a Baptist church, and a Presbyterian church. Because Georgetown wanted its own parish, the parish on the Black River was divided in 1734. The upper half was named Prince Frederick, and the lower half Prince George. Preparation began in Georgetown for a parish church. The beautiful Prince George Church there was completed in 1753.

The Episcopalians living on the Waccamaw wanted their own parish and church, since they had to ferry across the Waccamaw and Black rivers to worship. They petitioned the State Council, and an act was passed in 1767 creating All Saints Parish. A church was built on land given by the Pawley family which abutted River Road near Waverly Mills and Chapel Creek, so communicants could come by land or water.

Now if anyone in Waccamaw country wants to spend a delightful day and go back into church history, he should pack a lunch, visit the pretty 1753 Prince George Church in Georgetown, then drive about sixteen miles on Highway 51 towards Brown's Ferry and see the churchyard of Prince George Winyah, the mother church of the entire Pee Dee section of South Carolina. It is on a horseshoe bend of the Black River and is one of the prettiest sites in South Carolina. After rice was being planted on the Pee Dee River and more people were living in this area, the church was moved to Plantersville near the Pee Dee River and was called the Gunn Church after the name of the builder. Near the site of the original churchyard on the Black River is the site of an old Presbyterian church erected in 1727 and called Black Mingo or the Old Brick Church. This church was burned by the British during the Revolution, but the old cemetery remains on a hill near the county line road dividing Georgetown and Williamsburg counties. While you are in this area you

Old Belin Baptist Church near Black Mingo Creek.

should go about five miles farther and see the Old Belin Baptist Church near Black Mingo Creek. This church was given by another member of the Belin family who was a merchant and planter in the area and whose name was Cleland Belin. The church is perfectly square, made of wood, and has Bible verses carved in the wide boards just under the roof.

It is unusual that these two men who were cousins from the same French Huguenot heritage should both endow churches of different denominations in the same general vicinity. It is also strange that the family of Belin who had many plantations on the Waccamaw, Black, and Pee Dee rivers should no longer have any heirs by that name.

7

RUM GULLY TALES

Many is the night young and old have gathered after supper on the porch at Tuck'em Inn to spin and listen to yarns of the coastal area. There were pirate stories, sea stories, murder stories, ghost stories, fish stories, love stories, and an occasional true story.

A favorite with the children was a story about a family of porpoises that lived in Murrells Inlet. The family consisted of Joe Porpoise the father, Della Porpoise the mother, children Joe, Jr., Sam Crawford, and their sister Elizabeth. They heard how the father had to work at the business of catching fish to feed his family; how he loved to take trips and would come by the end of the pier in Main Creek and blow for our children to come take a ride with him. They would get on his back and away they would go—past Rum Gully Swash to see Don Bigby, up Main Creek to see how many fishermen were on the government pier, then into Parsonage Creek to go by Thalia Salmons and perhaps stop for a few minutes to get a hamburger or some other goody.

Summer holidays were Joe's favorites. He never missed the Fourth of July boat parade at Murrells Inlet, an outstanding show with over a hundred decorated boats participating. He was there when the parade began in the Sunnyside section and followed it for several miles before hundreds of decorated houses and yards filled with spectators. He also checked on Billy and Adele Hewitt's annual picnic that day.

On Labor Day he hustled down to Garden City for the midday party hosted by Bunnie and Jimmy Johnson and Tom and Ann Stackhouse.

Some nights Joe took his own children to the porpoise school where they learned to catch fish. The correct method was to knock the fish out with a slap of the tail and then catch them to eat. If they were real smart, they would slap the fish up in the air and catch it in their mouths before it fell in the water. The porpoise children were taught to eat the best fish such as mullet, yellow tails, and croakers and to beware of the catfish with its sharp barbs and the jellyfish with its poisonous discharge.

In self-defense classes, the porpoise children learned that their best weapon was their strong nose. To attack a shark or other mean fish, they should swim at full speed and ram that nose hard into a vulnerable spot just behind their opponent's eye or gill. Our children seemed to love these stories, and children from nearby cottages would come to hear them.

Sometimes Joe Porpoise would ask his passengers to take a lunch because they were going as far as Myrtle Beach to see the tall new hotel Mr. Woodside was erecting or to Pawleys Island to see if they could spot the Gray Man roaming in the dunes. These porpoise stories were legend, and the children would not go to bed until they had heard a new adventure of the Porpoise family.

Our own true porpoise story occurred when Suzanne and I went fishing near Beach Landing in our eight-foot dink. We had just thrown out the anchor and started fishing, when this very large porpoise came up to the boat, gave us a shove with his nose, and continued to push our little boat around. Suzanne got so nervous and excited, she insisted that we move. When we had settled down to fishing about a mile away, the same porpoise came along and nudged the side of the boat. By this time Suzanne was frantic, and we had to stop fishing and go home. I will always believe that the bright yellow play suit she was wearing at-

Sunnyside, built by J. Motte Alston in 1885, now owned by Mrs. Mary Walker.

tracted the porpoise. Because he seemed to like bright colors, we gave him a name and that name was Joe. Sound familiar?

We heard many times the story of Dr. Smiley Bigham and his landlord who killed Mrs. Bigham to prevent her testifying in the murder trial of the doctor's brother Edmund. She had put on a white beach robe to go swimming just before dark on the beach in front of Sunnyside House. The men said they had thought she was a ghost and had shot her.

No one could tell this story as well as Jim Heyward whose brother Wallace was working at Sunnyside the same night she was killed. He would tell how, when he heard the shot, he ran to the edge of the water and found Mrs. Bigham dying. He helped her up to the house and laid her on the front porch. He told about her blood which was running down on the steps. You can see the stain from it to this day. And on a clear evening just before dark with a waning moon, you might see her walking near the water's edge.

Then there was the tale of the man who was in the creek

looking for stone crabs. He put his hand and arm down a large crab hole, and something very strong caught his hand and wouldn't let go. He was held there until the tide came in and he drowned. On certain nights when the tide and moon are just right, you can hear him cry for help.

There was the tale about Arch Pickett, a former creek boy at the Inlet, who lost his sight in a hunting accident. He knew the creeks so well he could walk in them, day or night, with a pitchfork and prog for flounders. He lived to a ripe old age and died from natural causes.

Peggy Hall had a story about her Grandmother Buck, who was living in the house at Bucks Landing at the Inlet during the famous hurricane of 1893. The water came so high and the wind blew so hard for days that they moved all they could to the second floor, then endured the storm.

Water covered the first floor and rose almost to the top of the stairway. After the storm had blown out and the water had receded, she asked the servants to take a survey of the damage. They reported that the chicken houses had been washed away and the chickens drowned, the tools were gone, but the main house seemed to be all right. While bemoaning the loss of their chickens, they heard cackling above their heads. All of the chickens were perched on the peak of the second-story roof and impatient to come down and be fed.

We often had to tell about the Rum Gully Telephone Company. One of our best operators was Hattie Bell Bigby who lived across Rum Gully Swash from Tuck'em Inn. To get a message to the other side of the swash, we would yell it to Hattie Bell, who would relay the message to her sister Ann Wilson Powell, who would pass it on.

Hattie Bell visited the Inlet often as a girl and enjoyed the breeze, the good seafood, and the waterfront gossip. After she married Clarence Bigby, she persuaded him and their son Don to vacation at the Inlet. Clarence complained about the sand flies and mosquitoes and became so disgusted that they went home in a week.

The next summer the Bigbys were back. Apparently the mosquitoes and flies did not bite so bad, for they purchased a lot on Rum Gully Swash and built a house. When they moved to Litchfield Beach some years and several houses later, the Rum Gully Telephone Company was never the same. Only Hattie Bell had that perfect pitch and tone to get a message across the swash.

More stories were told about Theodosia Burr, the beautiful and talented daughter of Aaron Burr and wife of the young and handsome Governor of South Carolina Joseph Alston, who lived at the Oaks, a plantation just beyond Brookgreen. You remember she left Georgetown on the pilot schooner *Patriot* bound for New York to meet her father who had been exiled and who was returning to America after a three-year absence. The schooner was never heard from again. Perhaps pirates captured the ship and forced the crew to walk the plank. A better story was that the pirate captain was young and handsome and fell in love with beautiful Theodosia. He persuaded her to go with him and live in the pirates' Shangri-la at the lost city of Port Royal on the island of Jamaica.

Another story was that her former sweetheart, the young and famous portrait painter John Vanderlyn, then living in South America, had the *Patriot* captured off the North Carolina coast by a privateer. He took Theodosia to live with him forever after in Guatemala. The most probable story was that her ship was in a violent storm near Cape Hatteras and driven ashore. All the passengers and crew drowned, and the ship was beaten to pieces on the rocks. One story was that a young and beautiful woman was washed ashore on the Outer Banks holding on to a painting. Though she had lost her memory, a family on the Outer Banks nursed her and took care of her until she died. She was later identified as Theodosia by the beautiful portrait discovered hanging in a fisherman's cabin.

Then there was the true story of the man who built a fence across the main channel near the mouth of the Inlet. At the incoming tide he would open the gates wide to let the fish in, and at high tide, he closed them to trap the fish so that he would always have plenty.

Once people thought they heard cannon shots near the mouth of the Inlet, and upon investigating, found a whale grounded on a sandbar in shallow water. He was slapping the water so hard with his tail in an effort to get off the bar, it sounded like cannon fire. Then there was the night we were sitting on the porch at Tuck'em Inn and heard loud splashing out in the water. When we went out on the pier with a flashlight, we found the whole Inlet full of a school of spotted rays which had come in with the tide. They were so thick you dared not swim or wade for fear of being stung.

Paul Wesley told about the time he was fishing for sharks near the mouth of the Inlet. A large fish took his bait and, securely hooked, pulled him out into the ocean. The fish was so large and pulled him so far that it was two days before he could row back to shore.

Another good story is about Captain Charlie Leonard who in about 1910 was the first person to take people out fishing for a fee on his twenty-foot Seabright skiff with a one-cylinder Lathrop engine. He used Woodland Creek to come in and go out, and at that time it was so winding you had to go a mile or more to get back where you started. To save time and gas, Captain Charlie hired some workmen with shovels and at low tide they dug a ditch or canal through the marsh from one bend of the creek to another. This started the water flowing through, and the tide and flow of water continued to widen and deepen the cut. It is now used by everyone and known as Charlie's Cut.

In the late twenties there was a new pavilion at Myrtle Beach with a large dance floor and concession stands, and they began contracting popular bands to play for weekend and mid-week dances.

One of the good tales to come out of this period was that a group of Marion boys who were staying at the Inlet attended a Saturday night dance at the pavilion. Maybe they

The first pavilion at Myrtle Beach.

had been sipping on persimmon beer or home brew, but after the dance they decided to take a swim in the surf. Thinking that all the people had gone home, they proceeded to undress on the beach and go in the water. They had hardly gotten wet when they heard a siren, and several spotlights focused on them. A loudspeaker blared them out of the water. When they came up on the beach, the police demanded a fine of twenty-five dollars each or a trip to jail. They didn't have that much money and began arguing with the officers to reduce the fine. The policemen were firm, but they also knew that the Myrtle Beach jail was not large enough to hold so many boys and that they would have to give them breakfast. During the argument Malcolm Woods, a promising young attorney, came to see what was causing the excitement. The boys knew him and engaged him to represent them. After much dickering back and forth, Malcolm got the fine reduced to $1.50 each.

The swimmers hurriedly found their clothes and paid their fines and left for the Inlet. I don't think Malcolm collected much of a fee from this case, but his reputation as a lawyer and negotiator was made.

8

HIAWATHA AT THE HERMITAGE

The first outdoor drama in the Carolinas was performed at Murrells Inlet in 1915. A splendid account of the event was written for the Horry County Historical Society by Genevieve Willcox Chandler, and we rely on that impeccable source. Mrs. Chandler took a major role in the drama and was the daughter of Mrs. Clarke Willcox, Sr., the adapter, planner, and director of this ambitious project to assist the local school.

After the school at the Inlet burned in 1914, Mr. "Doc" Spivey of Conway donated an acre for a new building. This property was virgin forest and the cost of clearing was great. Many live oaks had to be cut down.

In 1915 Henry Willcox, chairman of the school board of trustees, went to Georgetown by steamship and informed the "powers that be" that valuable future citizens on Waccamaw Neck needed a new schoolhouse. Money was appropriated, and a two-room building was erected. Sliding doors allowed for a community gathering place when needed.

Tree stumps, however, dotted the entire playground. The school authorities had not promised to beautify the yard. Though school boys dug vigorously before school and at recess, they clearly needed help. Estimates were made.

"We need money," said Genevieve to her mother.

"What for?"

"To stump the school yard."

"Well," she said, "let's give a play. Aren't the children studying *Hiawatha*? Aren't they interested in collecting artifacts? We'll have a show. We'll give *Hiawatha*!"

We were standing on the porch of the Hermitage, my mother's home. She looked toward the grove. "We have the dark and gloomy forest, the pines with cones upon them."

Dramatically spreading her arms wide, she pointed north to Vereen's Fishery. She pointed south to Lachicotte's canning factory. The inlet spread before us, the high tide flooding the marsh.

"There," she said, "is the Big-Sea-Water! Here is Gitche Gumee!"

And so our Hiawatha was conceived.

(Today Surfside is where Vereen's Fishery was. Huntington Beach is at Magnolia near Lachicotte's canning factory.)

Without delay Mama ordered Indian music. A book of songs recorded on Indian reservations soon arrived. We opened it and read:

"Yah! Hah! Hah!
Yah he dub liah!"

"Well, Sister," she said, "You teach the words, and I'll teach the music."

The words were copied on the blackboard at school. This was a new language, and we worked hard.

The children went home from school and reported that Miss Minnie was going to have a show and everyone who wanted to be in it should come to the schoolhouse Friday night. Whole families came. As Alice Outlaw Owens of Socastee said after over half a century, "We knew if Miss Minnie was doing it, it would turn out right. She can make something out of nothing."

In 1915 the Inlet had no telephone, radio, or movie.

Funerals were the only occasion on which we gathered ourselves together—except, of course, for Sabbath services. Meeting at the schoolhouse after a week of hard work was relaxing. We really pleasured ourselves. We sang lustily. The braves-to-be memorized pages of Longfellow's beautiful poetry, and the words of the Indian songs mattered not. Maybe translated they would mean, "Paint your faces. We are going on the warpath." But they had rhythm!

There were tedious hours when the actors accented the wrong word. I remember Mrs. Emma Oliver's saying, "Mrs. Willcox, tell 'em to mock you!" and, born mimics, mock her they did.

When Ira Vick, Hermon and Clifton Wilson, Cliff Johnson and his brother, Charlie Strickland, John and Jim Causey, Gustavus Ludlow, and their friends dressed in clam-sack shirts embellished with seashells, bits of shiny tin foil, and yellow, red, and brown cheesecloth fringe, it seemed to the beholder that long-gone aborigines were before us.

Mama wrote her own script. Carefully reading the poem she selected the scenes to be portrayed. She perfectly cast her characters. She made weird music on Grandma's eighteenth-century Mason and Hamlin organ. With one fiddler (my brother Dr. Allston Willcox, who "played it by air") and homemade tom-toms giving the beat, the Indian braves singing and cavorting around a big bonfire under the live oaks and moss were almost terrifying!

Sitting on the front porch with needle and thimble, Mama designed and made almost a hundred costumes for those who came faithfully each week to practice. She was impressed with Lee Outlaw from Socastee who, on occasion, worked his crops all day, then walked to the creek for Friday night's workout—eight miles! Alice Outlaw Owens wrote to me, "As I remember, we practiced almost a year!" It was our great endeavor for a long winter to get ready for "next summer and full moon."

In scene one, Mrs. P. Herbert Wesley as old Nokomis made a dramatic entrance with her real grandson strapped

The entire cast of the outdoor drama staged at the Hermitage, Murrells Inlet, 1915 and 1916.

in a cradle board on her back. Wrapped in her grandmother's paisley shawl brought from England, she removed the cradle board, hung it from a gargoyle-shaped burl on a centuries-old oak. The audience thought it was a doll baby. When the baby rolled his eyes and turned his head, they whispered, "He is alive!"

The baby's eight-year-old brother portrayed Hiawatha as a boy and sang the beautiful firefly song:

"Wah-Wah-taysee, little firefly,
Little flitting white-fire insect,
Light me with your little candle,
Ere upon my bed I lay me,
Ere in sleep I close my eyelids!"

Things were so timed that as the full moon rose from the water, Hiawatha pointed and whispered:

"What is that, Nokomis?"
And she answered:

The pageant at Murrells Inlet, 1915. From left to right, Minnehaha, Mrs. Genevieve Chandler; Arrow-Maker, Captain Charlie Leonard; Mrs. W.L. Hewitt, Sr., and Clarke Willcox, Jr., who played Hiawatha.

"Once a warrior, very angry,
Seized his grandmother, and threw her
up into the sky at midnight;
Right against the moon he threw her;
'Tis her body that you see there."

Wigwams were erected under the eight-acre oak grove. Each Indian family had a fire before their teepee. Some, realistically, had their hound dogs. To the extreme right was the "land of the Dakotas." Here Charlie Leonard sat before his teepee perfectly cast as the ancient Arrow-Maker. Minnehaha was by his side. This teepee was in darkness until a spotlight followed Hiawatha going to see his bride.

To me the most impressive scene was when Dalrymple Johnson, trained in law at Princeton University, appeared as Gitche Manito, the mighty. His descent to earth was so arranged that to the spectators it seemed as great a mystery as the coming of the great spirit seemed to the Indians that Longfellow portrayed. Across the end of the avenue behind the cleared space of the stage, my mother had had planted rows of pine saplings as a background. An inclined plane starting at the treetops was the ladder down which Gitche Manito descended from heaven. For his headdress, our cook's sons had caught our geese one by one and Mama, with a pair of large shears, had clipped their wings to make his white war bonnet, a thing of beauty and mystery.

Mr. Johnson's words rolled out as he fairly preached a sermon to the Indians:

"Oh, my children! my poor children!
I am weary of your quarrels,
Of your wranglings and dissensions;"

He promised:

"I will send a Prophet to you.
Bury your war-clubs and your weapons,
Smoke the calumet together
And as brothers live henceforward!"

He kept his promise. Hiawatha, coming of age, was the prophet. He developed Indian corn for their food. Mondamin, the spirit of corn, was played by Miss Mittie Gibson of Vaux Hall—now Mrs. Leewood McCollum of Rowland, North Carolina. In filmy green draperies with her long golden hair like corn silk, she needed no wig. Hiawatha wrestled and overcame Mondamin and, as instructed, buried her in the earth from which grew a stalk of corn to provide food for his nation.

Remembering Minnehaha, whom he had seen as a youth,

Hiawatha left for a journey to the "land of the Dakotas."
Old Nokomis warned:

"Bring not to my lodge a stranger
from the land of the Dakotas!
Very fierce are the Dakotas,
Often is there war between us."

Unheeding, Hiawatha replied:

"As unto the bow the cord is,
So unto the man is woman,
Though she bends him, she obeys him,
Though she draws him, yet she follows,
Useless each without the other!"

The spotlight followed Hiawatha's arrival bearing a gift of a deer which he laid at the feet of his beloved. Minnehaha went to Hiawatha saying, "I will follow you, my husband." The spotlight returned to Nokomis preparing the wedding feast.

This wedding feast was probably the most exciting scene of the play with all of the bonfires lighted and every teepee occupied. The entire cast was present.

Firelight from many wigwams played on the curtains of waving moss. Around a great black wash pot (Spanish browned for the occasion) Pau-Puk-Keewis danced wildly, Iagoo told one of his marvelous tales, and Chibiabos, the sweet singer sang, "Onaway! Awake, beloved!"

The famine scene followed. Mrs. Wesley in her paisley shawl searched beneath the oaks for acorns and prayed to Gitche Manito for food for the dying Minnehaha.

"Oh the famine and the fever!
Oh the wailing of the children!
Oh the anguish of the women!"

Children took an active part in the drama.

While Hiawatha was searching desperately for game, a bitter snow fell among the oaks. This miracle was assisted by Mrs. Napoleon Lafayette Vick, chief of the group of mothers and grandmothers who, sitting before their fires on winter evenings, had cut snippets of tissue paper and old newspaper by the barrel full. A director from Boston visiting the Inlet had told Mama how to make a snowstorm. Chuck Alford and other volunteer carpenters had built platforms high in the live oaks where men with the barrels of paper and cooperative breezes showered snow on the sad scenes far below. Oh, that we could have had movies of this beautiful picture!

When Hiawatha, exhausted from the hunt, entered his wigwam, he saw two uninvited guests, Fever and Famine, seated at the head and foot of their victim Minnehaha's bed of branches and moss. The artist of Indian life and customs, Frederic Remington, once illustrated Longfellow's poem and

HIAWATHA

July 28th at 8:30 p. m.

PROLOGUE

Gitche Manito appears and promises a prophet.
Hiawatha is born.

Scene I—Papoose and old Nokomis.
Scene II—Hiawatha's youth.
Scene III—Hiawatha's fasting—Appearance of Mondamin —Wrestling and victory of Hiawatha.
Scene IV—Hiawatha's wooing.
Scene V—Wedding feast.
Scene VI—Snowstorm, famine and death of Minnehaha.
Scene VII—Arrival of priest and departure of Hiawatha.

CAST—87 CHARACTERS.

HIAWATHA: Baby Morse, Laurie Morse, Clark Willcox, Jr.

Nokomis	Mrs. P. H. Wesley
Gitche Manito	Mr. W. D. Johnson
Mondamin	Miss Mittie Gibson
Iagoo	Jim Willcox
Paupukkeewis	Charlie Strickland
Chibiabos	Dr. J. C. Gasque
Arrow-Maker	Charley Leonard
Arrow-Maker's Daughter	Miss Genevieve Willcox
Fever	Miss Gibson
Famine	Mrs. J. C. Gasque
Priest	Dr. A. M. Willcox
Indian Princess	Miss Versa Vick

Explanatory Readers.

Miss Flossie Outlaw	Mr. Ira Vick
Miss Esther Vick	Mr. Jim Causey
Miss Florence Oliver	Captain Morse
Miss Versa Vick	Mr. Clifton Wilson
Mrs. G. E. Morse	Mr. Hermon Wilson
Mr. John Causey	Mr. Willie Oliver
Mr. Gus Ludlow	Mr. Bryan Johnson

The program printed here shows the scenes.

1. Prologue by Indian Men.
11. The Infant.
111. The Youthful Hiawatha.
1V. Hiawatha Reaching Manhood, Struggles with Mondamin Getting Indian Corn.
V. HE GOES TO THE LAND OF THE DAKOTAS FOR MINNEHAHA
V1. WEDDING FEAST.
V11. TIME OF FAMINE
V111. MINNEHAHA'S DEATH.
1X. COMING OF WHITE MAN
X. HIAWATHA DEPARTS TO THE "LAND OF THE HEREAFTER."

Program for the pageant, Hiawatha.

painted Fever and Famine who filled one with horror. My mother disagreed and made them ghostly, but beautiful, white-draped spirits who danced in the flickering firelight an unearthly dance of death. Miss Mittie Gibson and Mrs. Laurie W. Gasque performed in marvelous fashion.

Offshore from the Hermitage grove is a little shell island, supposedly made centuries ago by many an Indian oyster roast and clam bake. It rises above high tide and shows white and ghostly above the marsh. As this full moon shed its light over the marshes, a canoe could be seen on the beach facing the island. Now the Indians en masse followed Hiawatha to the water's edge, for he was leaving to join his beloved in "the land of the Hereafter."

Stepping into this birch canoe Hiawatha whispered, "Westward! Westward!" Like a murmur from the sea came the Indian voices: "Farewell, O Hiawatha!" The soughing pines joined, "Farewell Hiawatha!" And the little waves upon the margin sobbed, "Farewell, O Hiawatha!" Arms uplifted, Hiawatha stood, as mysteriously the canoe glided across the moonlit waters.

No one could see Vance Hewitt hidden in the bushes on the shell island gently winding in an invisible wire! This was magic! One spectator was heard to say, as departing guests boarded wagons and carts to go home after the play, "The purtiest part was where that thar canoe just moved away with nary an oar, paddle, or motor. Jist vanished in the marshes!"

The second summer the play was given, I was only seven years old, but remember it well: the Kaminskis sent their yacht carrying people from Georgetown, and the steamboat *Ruth* arrived with guests from Conway. Every cottage on the Inlet was overflowing with guests, and Tuck'em Inn lived up to its name with two or more in every bed and people sleeping on cots and hammocks. Many arrived in rowboats from various inlets and coves, and the local population came in wagons lighted by lanterns hanging beneath. Thanks were offered to many, who, at one point in the play, formed a semicircle with their cars and flooded the scene with headlights as brilliantly as footlights in a theater.

As many said, "Miss Minnie had made sumpin' outer nothin," and it is uncanny what memories linger of the Inlet show in which almost one hundred percent of a village cooperated amicably. And thus the school yard was stumped!

By the following year Hiawatha was on the way to France with the Rainbow Division, and Minnehaha was an ambulance driver with the American Red Cross in the war zone.

Recently I asked Levi Hewitt if he remembered the pageant. He rushed in the house and returned with a worn photograph of an Indian family in front of their wigwam. "You see that papoose?" he said. "That baby is Levi Hewitt."

9

HIGH SCHOOL DAYS AT THE INLET

In the fall of 1922 my parents decided to winterize Tuck'em Inn. They planned to close in the screened living room with windows and build a new room with a large fireplace and chimney.

Arthur Evans was again engaged to do the carpentry work and Buck Davis to do the masonry. I took them to the Inlet during the Christmas holidays and stayed to run errands and go for supplies. I invited Custis Moore to go along thinking we could get in some hunting.

The work progressed nicely in spite of the cold weather, and we killed a duck or two and some birds to add variety to Arthur's cooking. As the only heat in the house was the wood stove in the kitchen, we gathered there after supper to play setback, or stealing casino.

One afternoon about three o'clock a couple of local farmers drove into the yard in a two-horse wagon. They had been fishing for mullet on the beach, and there had been a man in a small boat anchored about a mile from shore. They said he had waved to them the first two days, but they could see no signs of life today with the weather getting colder and the wind stronger and felt they should report it.

We took them to the Smiths in the car to tell Luther and ask him to tow in the boat. We drove to the beach and saw the boat, but no sign of anyone in it.

The wind was blowing strong from the northwest and it was getting very cold. Luther Smith didn't think the man could survive the night. Since it was too rough to take a boat out of the inlet, he decided to try to launch a small boat through the surf. Howard Wesley volunteered to row. He was about eighteen years old and had been handling boats all of his life.

By the time we found a seaworthy skiff, loaded it up, and reached the beach, it was getting dark. Howard wore a life jacket and carried a blanket to wrap up the man. All of us put the boat with Howard in it on our shoulders to carry it beyond the breakers.

It was nip and tuck to get him through the waves without swamping in the high seas. Finally we watched him row out of sight. We built a big fire on the beach with driftwood to keep warm and show Howard where to come ashore. After a long wait wondering if Howard would make it, we heard a yell and waded into the water to get the boat ashore.

Howard was exhausted and soaking wet, and the blanket-covered man in the bottom of the boat looked more dead than alive. Two men helped him to the fire. Another forced some brandy or corn whiskey down his throat.

The men in the wagon were left to bring back the skiff, and we took our stranger to the Smiths and went for a doctor.

He recovered in a few days and told us that he was a Mr. Simkins from Georgetown and had gone on the ocean or outside route to Wilmington on business. Since there was no inland waterway at that time, he had left Southport with a couple of sandwiches and a thermos of water, and his engine had broken down near Surfside. He had anchored the boat and waved to the fishermen for help, but they had just waved back. He was very grateful for our help. Howard was later awarded a medal for his part. Luther brought the boat in after the weather had improved, and Mr. Simkins had the motor repaired and left for Georgetown.

Custis and I stayed until the room was finished and returned to school full of tales.

The next summer Jack Bates called me to say that he and Gus Kaminer were bringing horses to the Inlet and would bring one for me, stopping in Marion to pick me up.

The boys stayed with me, and we left on horseback early the next morning for the Inlet. We rode all day and spent the night with a family of Coopers between Aynor and Conway.

The next day we arrived at the Inlet and the horses were stabled behind the Bates' cottage. Ducky cooked for us and caught fish and other seafood. The standard menu was fish, grits, and beets from the Bates farm with a breakfast of scrambled eggs or crab cakes.

We rode as far north as Myrtle Beach and as far south as Pawleys Island. One afternoon we were invited to the Lachicottes' farm to visit some girls and have supper. We stabled the horses in a barn near the house. After dark when we were ready to go home, Jack went in the barn to get the horses. Out he sailed as if he had been shot from a cannon. It seems that the farm hands had come in after we did, moved our horses, and put mules in those stalls. Jack met the rear of a farm mule and was kicked on both shins. He had no broken bones but was sore and black and blue for several weeks.

Another time we rode the horses to Carson's store for some groceries, and it was my lot to carry the eggs. Returning through a swampy area, I was holding the eggs in one hand and the reins in the other. The horse bolted because of a snake, and I turned loose the eggs to hold the horse. Every one of the eggs was broken. We did without eggs for a whole week.

We sometimes rode over to visit Dr. Ward Flagg who was living in the old kitchen at Brookgreen plantation. He would tell us stories about when he was a boy and would sometimes give us a glass of homemade wine from the many bottles in his wine locker. He told us that most of the wine was brought to him by his patients in thanks for taking care of them.

That summer a Boy Scout troop camped in back of the Mood cottage. Their scoutmaster owned the Palmetto Pigeon Farm in Sumter and had written the national merit badge requirements for pigeon raising. We got to know Edward Buck, Henry Shelor, Pootie Averbuck, and Randolph Guthrie who became a New York lawyer and senior partner in the law firm with Mitchell and Nixon. Charles Green, the bugler, awakened us each morning with reveille played so well you really wanted to get up.

Our neighbor Colonel J. Monroe Johnson, purchased a new sixteen-foot outboard skiff that summer and had it shipped by freight to Conway. He asked me to bring it down the Waccamaw River for him. We had a new Johnson five-horsepower outboard motor with alternate firing which was really the first outboard on the market that would surely run and almost always get you home.

I invited the Colonel's nephew Palmer and my younger brother Jack to go along. Colonel Johnson took us to Conway with extra gas, life cushions, and a good lunch. We launched the boat behind the Jerry Cox Company's store and headed to Wachesaw Landing behind the Inlet. It was a beautiful summer day with the river almost begging us to come along and share its beauty. The boat and motor were behaving perfectly.

We decided to play cooter poker which is the Waccamaw version of car poker we had played in automobiles many times. Pam and Jack each chose a side of the river on which to count cooters. The rule was that an alligator on your side canceled all of your cooters and you had to begin counting again.

There must have been a turtle convention on the Waccamaw that day for there were sometimes ten to twenty cooters on each log and the Rum Gully computer was busy trying to keep up with numbers. Pam was over one hundred ahead when we reached Bucksville, then Jack spotted an alligator on Pam's side of the river, and he had to begin counting all over. It was nip and tuck for there were thousands of cooters and eight or ten alligators spotted on our way down the river. Just before we passed Prince Creek below Bucksport, Pam saw a gator on Jack's side that was too close to Wachesaw for Jack to recoup. As the loser, Jack had to buy the Coca-Colas at Willcox's store when we reached the Inlet.

Andrew Keith met us and we loaded boat, motor, and gear aboard his oxcart. At Tuck'em Inn we snuggled in our beds with visions not of sugarplums but cooters in our heads.

On New Year's Day in 1924 Frank Salmon called me. "Pratt, we must make some New Year's resolutions and I must see you right away." Wondering whether Frank had in mind to stop having dates or eating oysters or tinkering with his car, I hurried to his house to hear the good or bad news. His resolution was that we must spend more time at Murrells Inlet during the coming year.

Spending at least one weekend a month at the Inlet seemed feasible. Since we were both working and going to school, it meant leaving Marion after work on Saturday night, driving to the Inlet, spending Sunday there, and coming back Sunday afternoon. Frank was working at Byars Motor Company, and I was working at Schell Drug Store. We both had Model T Ford stripdowns and could carry several boys with us in each car. Mine was a 1913 model with a brass-head radiator for which I had paid thirty-five dollars, and Frank had a 1918 model that he and Lawrence Murden had put together out of junk and spare parts. Both cars had windshields but no top, one wide seat in front, and a box on the back which would seat one or two persons.

Our usual weekend crowd besides Frank and me included Lawrence, Bob Jones, S.J. Salmon, Henry Mullins, Skeeter Solomon, and John Cross. Custis Moore was away at school in Virginia. We did a little fishing, played a little penny poker and setback, and even taught Henry and Frank the manly art of washing dishes.

Some trips were uneventful; on others we would have trouble with the cars or an unusual number of flat tires, but Lawrence was a good mechanic and we carried plenty of spare tires and tubes. The usual flat-tire procedure was for S.J. or Lawrence, our strong boys, to lift up the wheel while one of us placed a block of wood under the axle so the tire could be removed. Our two cars traveled together so we always had plenty of help.

What made travel difficult on sandy roads was that in the 1920s the automobile companies changed the wheel gauges on their cars, making them a foot narrower. Now you would have two wheels in the old rut and have to blaze a new trail with the other wheels. This burned out many a low gear on the Model T Fords.

Once during duck season Lawrence roused S.J. just before daybreak on Sunday morning to tell him there were some ducks in Rum Gully Swash and if he would quietly slip around the house and crawl on his stomach to the sea wall, he could get a good shot. S.J. loaded his double-barreled gun and crawled to the sea wall through the cactus and sand spurs. We were all watching from the window as S.J. raised up and let go at the ducks with both barrels. Captain Buxton's wooden decoys turned over and over in the water. Lawrence never did confess to knowing they were decoys all along. Then we worried about damage to Captain Buck's wooden ducks.

There were no houses on the beach across from the Inlet, and we often sailed over there to look for shells, swim, or play ball. One warm day Henry Mullins, Jack Bates, and I decided to go swimming without bathing suits. We swam, played leapfrog on the beach, and rode the waves, then dressed and sailed back to Curlew Point. Mr. Henry Buck was sitting on his porch with a powerful new telescope. He told us in great detail about our activities of the afternoon.

One spring day in late April, I found a note on my desk calling a meeting of the Murrells Inlet group at first recess. We decided that with the good weather and with exams coming up, we needed a week's rest at Murrells Inlet to prepare us for the ordeal. In addition to our usual crowd, we invited Ed Bell and Wilton Stevenson to go with us.

Somehow we got our parents' permission and the use of Tuck'em Inn. The merchants of Marion were having Golden Rule Sales on the first Monday in May, and the filling stations were selling five gallons of gasoline for one dollar. We decided to fill the stripdowns with gas at the sale and not use them until we started on our trip the next weekend.

One of the cars was parked in the barn behind the Cross house, and one morning at school John Cross told us that the tank was leaking and our bargain gas was seeping away. That night we spent draining and fixing the tank, but we saved all but two gallons of fuel.

The trip was so well planned that we even talked some of the girls in our crowd into having a house party on the next weekend. They persuaded Mrs. James Johnson to come down with them and stay at Vaux Hall. In the group were Elizabeth McIntyre, Reubie Holliday, Lenora Monroe, Hattie Bell Bethea, and Mary Sale from Mullins.

The week was a great success. We caught fish, swam on the beach, toured the Grand Strand, and all went to a dance at the new hotel at Floral Beach (now Surfside). Since Reubie's father was the hotel owner and developer of the beach, we expected to get a free ticket to the dance, but no soap. We all paid and even had to buy a ticket for Reubie. Her father, George Holliday of Galivants Ferry, had renamed Floral Beach for his wife Flora when he bought it from C.A. Roach. A few lots had sold and development had begun. They had built a hotel back in the sand dunes and had weekend dances during the summer. It looked as if Floral Beach was going to be a success, but the local economy was not good, crops were selling cheap, Mr. Holliday had other interests to distract him, and he did not push Floral Beach.

The next Wednesday a taxi drove up in the back yard of Tuck'em Inn and in walked Sam Woodberry with a message from our principal Colie Seaborn saying that if the seniors in our crowd expected to graduate from Marion High School in June, they had better get back to town and to classes. This meant Frank, Lawrence, Skeeter, and Ed Bell had to leave us.

The rest of us stayed on, even though our best cook, Lawrence Murden, was gone. John Cross was a good kitchen organizer and I could make pancakes and fry eggs, so we finished the week without mishap.

And we finished high school with many good memories of times at the Inlet.

10

MUD BANKS AND MONEY BANKS

Something at Murrells Inlet developed and inspired bankers. It may have been the good seafood, the water, or the Rum Gully School of Banking, but the Inlet produced more than its share of bankers.

Henry Mullins of Curlew Point was president of the old Bank of Marion and the Bank of Mullins. Howard Cross came to Marion with George Norwood to help run the new Marion National Bank and was later drafted to head the Farmers and Merchants Bank. Sam Norwood, son of George, followed in his father's footsteps at Marion National Bank, whose other presidents included James Johnson, summer resident in the house next to Vaux Hall; Bill Miles, who frequently visited the Hughes and Carmichael cottage; and Frank Salmon, my close friend who spent many weekends at Tuck'em Inn.

About 1924 when I was in high school, my friend Tom Craig called to say he would pick me up in Marion to go to the Inlet for a long weekend. In his Ford stripdown that trip was Olin Nesbit, who after finishing Davidson College, started the Interstate Securities Company. After Harvard Business School, Tom went with the New York brokerage firm of Dominick and Dominick.

Luther Byars in the Parsonage section of the Inlet became president of the Citizens Bank in Marion, and his daughter

Teedie Steadman is already a director of the Marion National Bank. Joel Smith III of Columbia is president of the South Carolina branch of the North Carolina National Bank. He's a son of Joe and Mary Lowndes Smith who visited Tuck'em Inn many times.

Just west of Tuck'em Inn, the W.K. Davises regularly entertained his brother and family of four boys. The oldest son Jack would head the State Planters Bank and Trust Company of Richmond, Virginia, and third son Archie would serve as chairman of the board of Wachovia Bank and Trust of Winston-Salem and be elected president of the American Bankers Association.

Hugh McColl, Sr., president of the Marlboro Trust Company in Bennettsville, rented the Hughes house and his three sons learned to calculate counting the sand fiddlers rather than fooling with computers. Hugh, Jr., is now chairman of the board and CEO of North Carolina National Bank. His brother Jimmie is a regional vice-president with Citizens and Southern National Bank, and Kenneth is a vice-president and loan officer with the South Carolina National in Greenville.

We don't even count all the bank directors such as Duncan McIntyre, Caroll Atkinson, Billy Nichols, McKoy Rose, Thomas Hunter, and so on.

I'd like to see organized the Fisherman's National Bank of Murrells Inlet with a board of directors consisting of Archie Davis of Winston-Salem, Hugh McColl, Jr. of Charlotte, Joel Smith III of Columbia, and Mickey Spillane of Murrells Inlet. Perhaps we had better add Chester Duke of Marion to keep on the good side of the Federal Reserve System, as he is on the board.

11

THE RICE INDUSTRY

At the beginning of the Revolutionary War the large Waccamaw landowners were growing indigo for export all over the world and some rice. The process of hulling rice was still done by hand, thus restricting the enormous production and export that would come with invention of the rice mill.

Gabriel Marion owned Laurel Hill plantation, and it's more than likely that General Francis Marion visited his brother there between attacks on the British or his hide-and-seek games with Colonel Banastre Tarleton and the redcoats. Another brother, Job, lived near the North Carolina border around Calabash and was apparently able to send current news to Francis, beginning with the battles at Lexington and Concord.

There is a story that Gabriel and other plantation owners supplied the Swamp Fox and his brigade on Snow Island, and it is definitely known that the British had a gunboat patrolling Bull Creek to intercept any American troop activity on the Pee Dee or Waccamaw rivers. We know that William Alston of Clifton plantation and William Allston of Brookgreen were both captains in Marion's brigade. When the British occupied Georgetown, they sent patrols up Waccamaw Neck to raid Murrells Inlet for salt and to disrupt Marion's support from the plantation owners. Salt from the Inlet was also spirited up the Pee Dee River to

Snow Island to supply Marion's men with this necessary commodity.

From the Revolutionary War to 1900 the growing of rice on the great plantations in and around the Inlet and Georgetown created a culture and a way of life that was only equalled, but not exceeded, by the royalty of Europe with their vast estates and castles.

In the 1850s and '60s the Georgetown district harvested over one-half of the rice grown in the United States. Carolina rice was known all over the world. There were great rice barons: the William Allstons, the Joshua Wards, the Horrys, the Pawleys, the Nesbits, the Westons, and others. Each plantation was almost an empire within itself with its hundreds of servants, beautiful manor houses, and summer residences on the coast. Many families also had homes in Georgetown or Charleston for business convenience or to enjoy the active social season. Some spent summers at northern resorts such as Saratoga Springs and Newport. It was at Newport that Joseph Alston met Theodosia Burr. Planters had their grand carriages with liveried coachmen and their eight- and ten-oared boats with uniformed oarsmen to take them and their guests up and down the Waccamaw, Pee Dee, and Black rivers to church, to visit, and to transport their white gold to mill and market. They built their churches so that they could be reached by boat, like All Saints on Chapel Creek and Prince Frederick on the Big Pee Dee.

Two things made the rice empires possible. First was the Great Planner who gave us our low-country rivers with a tidal rise and fall of fresh water so that the rice fields could be watered or drained at any time through a series of canals and gates they called trunks. It is told that a slave on one of the plantations invented the trunk, one of the great advances of its time.

Second was the mill for hulling and cleaning rice invented by Jonathan Lucas who was born in England near the small town of Ingremont on the Irish Sea. He was educated as

Slaves pounding rice before invention of the rice mill.

a millwright, and some accounts say that he invented a rice mill in England and some of our influential rice planters contacted him and asked him to come to America; others say that he came to America on a trip, saw opportunity for a good trade in this country, and stayed. Another tale was that his ship was wrecked near the mouth of the Santee River, and he came ashore to revive a struggling industry —definitely not a Jonah!

We do know that he built his first rice mill on the Santee River for John Bowman who was the son-in-law of Thomas Lynch of Hopsewee plantation, a signer of the Declaration of Independence.

This first mill was called a water mill as the water was impounded in a pond of higher elevation and turned the mill wheels as it ran to the lower levels. Soon after this, Lucas built a mill on Colonel Peter Horry's plantation, Belle Isle on Winyah Bay, and about 1791, another mill for Colonel William Alston on his Fairfield plantation on the Waccamaw. (This property is now a part of the Arcadia plantation. The rice mill at Fairfield was purchased in the 1920s by Henry Ford and re-erected in the Henry Ford Museum and Greenfield Village in Dearborn, Michigan.)

The old rice mill at Fairfield plantation was purchased by Henry Ford and is now in the Henry Ford Museum in Dearborn, Michigan.

During the war of 1812, Joseph Alston was governor of South Carolina, and many boatmen and sailors from Waccamaw Neck were manning American privateers which operated out of Charleston and Georgetown to attack British ships. Colonel Peter Horry had a summer house on North Island and visited a company of militia stationed there each day. Can't you hear him telling them how we whipped the British when he was fighting with Francis Marion during the Revolution? Colonel Horry had a young slave named Scipeo who rowed or sailed him from North Island to his plantation on the bay.

North and South islands on each side of the entrance to Winyah Bay were originally included in Winyah Barony, a tract of twelve-thousand acres of land along the bay granted in the eighteenth century to Landgrave Robert Daniel and immediately sold to Landgrave Thomas Smith. A landgrave was the nearest thing to royalty in this country. They were usually persons favored by the King.

Meanwhile Jonathan Lucas continued to build and improve his mills, soon inventing one operated by the tidal flow. He built the first one for Andrew Johnstone at Annandale plantation on the North Santee and another one for Henry Laurens at Mepkin plantation. His son Jonathan II soon joined his father in mill construction. He married Lydia Simons of Middleburg plantation and erected an improved mill there for his father-in-law. Jonathan II purchased Rice Hope on the North Santee, and this plantation stayed in the Lucas family until 1926 when it was sold to William Beach of New York.

The family moved their business activities to Charleston. One of them built a mansion on Calhoun Street, and the son purchased property in the Canonborough area and a mill on the Cooper River. The old wall of this mill is still in existence. The elder Jonathan built a mill on the Ashley River known as West Point Mill, operated first by tide and later by steam; the building is still standing and is being used by the Municipal Yacht Basin and the Chamber of Commerce.

The Lucas family built mills all over the Eastern United States, in England, Egypt, India, and anywhere rice was grown. Most of the machinery for these mills was made in Charleston. Accompanied by a local foreman, it was shipped on a sailing vessel to the site. One such foreman was Price Bee who went to Egypt to build and operate mills, staying for several years before returning to Charleston.

Jonathan Lucas died in 1821 and is buried in the churchyard of St. Lukes Cathedral in Charleston. Jonathan II returned to England at the request of the British government to build mills in London and Liverpool where he died and was buried. Some say he was knighted by the King for his contribution to the rice industry.

Nowhere in Georgetown County have I seen an historical marker about this remarkable man who contributed so much to the state and the rice-growing world. There is no picture of Jonathan Lucas in the Georgetown Rice Museum or the Georgetown Public Library.

The story goes that there were five New England

schooners loading at Bucksport for northern markets when the firing at Fort Sumter started off the Civil War. The Yankee skippers were so afraid that their ships were going to be seized that they didn't finish loading but hastened to get out of the Waccamaw River and Winyah Bay.

When the ports of Charleston and Georgetown were blockaded, General P.T.G. Beauregard, who was commanding officer in Charleston, ordered General Trapier in Georgetown to survey and report any inlets along the coast that blockade runners could come in and out of. The general reported that the North Santee Inlet had eight feet of water at high tide over the bar and Murrells Inlet had nine feet.

Blockade runners from Nassau and Bermuda came in with medicine, ammunition, and other supplies. From North Santee they had to go up the Santee to the Northeastern Railroad bridge near Lanes, between Florence and Charleston, and unload. From the warehouse there, supplies were carried by train wherever needed.

When they came into Murrells Inlet, blockade runners had to unload their cargo at Bucks Landing or Woodland, put it on wagons to Wachesaw Landing on the Waccamaw, load it on river boats to Mars Bluff so the Wilmington and Manchester Railroad could transport it to Confederate forces.

The plantation owners moved their families and slaves inland. Among them were the Westons to Conwayboro, Colonel Dan Jordan to Aiken, and some of the Allstons to near Cheraw. A few of the rice plantations were taken and damaged by Federal troops. But more important, the slaves were freed. This was the beginning of the end of the rice-growing era on Waccamaw Neck. Some of the rice planters continued to grow rice but their concentrated source of labor was gone. The most successful planters were those who pursued other interests as well.

North and South islands, for example, were acquired soon after the war by General Edward Porter Alexander, who had invested in railroads and banks, becoming president of the Georgia Railroad and Banking Company with head-

Vaux Hall, the summer home of the Vaux family who planted rice on Sandy Island.

quarters in Augusta. General Alexander planted rice on South Island and used both islands as a hunting preserve and a place for entertaining his influential friends.

One of his visitors was President Grover Cleveland who hunted on South Island as a guest of the famous Georgetown Palmetto Club in 1894. The club's cook, William McCray, received a gold watch from the President after his visit. The inscription read: "To my friend William McCray by your friend Grover Cleveland."

Several hurricanes put saltwater into the rice fields, but some rice continued to be grown until 1916. That year an especially destructive hurricane ruined the crops, and the last of the commercial growers went out of business. The only rice grown now is to feed the ducks.

12

THE LACHICOTTES OF WAVERLY MILLS

One of the most interesting families of Waccamaw country and one which contributed much to its culture and improvement was the Lachicottes. The family migrated to Haiti from France in 1690 and planted coffee and sugar on their plantation there. *La chicotte* means stumps or spurs jutting out of a range of hills, and presumably they named the plantation for the stumps that remained after the beautiful mahogany trees were cut to clear their land for crops.

In the slave rebellion on the island in 1792, the father Pierre Henri de La Chicotte was killed, but the mother and two children, hidden in sugar barrels, escaped on the first ship leaving, a schooner bound for Philadelphia. A British privateer stopped the ship en route and took the family's remaining jewels and personal possessions.

After arriving at Philadelphia, they made contact with friends, the de Caradeuce family at Cedar Hill plantation on the Wando River near Charleston. They remained there for a while, then moved to the Hermitage plantation near Savannah which was owned by the Marquis de Montalet whom they had known in Haiti or France. The children went to school in Charleston and Savannah.

The mother, Madame Marie Francois Rossinol de La Chicotte, as the name was then spelled, decided to return to Haiti and try to recover some of the family property left on their plantation. She was never heard from again, and it was thought that her ship was wrecked or captured by pirates or that she was killed in the continuing insurrection in Haiti.

Philip Rossinol de La Chicotte, son of Pierre and Marie, at the age of seventeen shipped out of Savannah on a sailing vessel bound for Wilmington, North Carolina. The ship was lost in a storm, and Philip, after clinging to some wreckage without food or water for several days, was picked up by a ship en route to Charleston.

Philip was the first of the family to arrive in the Waccamaw area. He changed the spelling of his name and instead of using Rossinol as his last name as would be expected, he called himself Philip Rossinol Lachicotte. He worked in Charleston for a few years at the West Point Rice Mill on the Ashley River to learn the milling business, then went to Brookgreen to operate a rice mill for Colonel John Joshua Ward, the largest and wealthiest rice planter in the district.

When the War Between the States began, Philip enlisted in a local company of militia. He was captured by a Yankee ship while defending a Southern blockade runner trying to make port either at the mouth of the Santee River or Murrells Inlet. After some time in a northern prison, he was released in an exchange of prisoners and returned to the Waccamaw area. While he was in the army and in prison, his family had moved to a plantation on the Black River near Choppee.

Upon his return, he again operated the rice mill at Brookgreen until it burned in 1867. He then served as engineer on a Pee Dee River steamboat named the *Addie* until it caught fire and was run aground in Thoroughfare Creek.

He operated a rice mill at Keithfield plantation for a short time, and in 1871, he purchased Waverly plantation and mill from Joseph Blythe Allston who had inherited it from

Waverly Mills, on Waverly Creek, was operated by the Lachicotte family from 1871 to 1915.

his father Joseph Waties Allston. The elder Allston had died while his son was still small, and his brother, Governor Robert F.W. Allston of Chicora Wood, had run Waverly for his nephews until they came of age.

Philip Rossinol Lachicotte was industrious and a good businessman. He successfully managed his plantation and mill and was a stockholder and president of Georgetown's first railroad, the Georgetown and Lanes Railroad, that connected with the main line at Lanes. He was also a member of the famous Georgetown Palmetto Club which entertained President Cleveland on his visit to Georgetown and South Island.

Among Philip's sons who stayed in the Waccamaw area were Louis Claud, St. Julian, and Francis Williams. Louis Claude planted rice at various plantations, grew produce, and operated a canning factory at Murrells Inlet. St. Julian was in the rice business with his brother Francis. Francis's son Arthur Herbert Lachicotte began the manufacture of the famous Pawleys Island hammocks and started the Hammock Shops, which recently celebrated their fiftieth year.

The Lachicottes were Catholics while living in Haiti and Charleston, but when the Waccamaw branch of the family moved to Waverly, there being no Catholic church nearby, they attended All Saints and Belin Methodist churches. Many of the descendants were and are active members of All Saints Church and some served on the vestry and held other offices.

I often visited Waverly as a boy and enjoyed exploring the old mill site and the early post office building and eating the delicious black figs that were growing near the plantation house.

A granddaughter of Francis W. Lachicotte, Mrs. Alberta Lachicotte Quattlebaum wrote a very popular book on the Georgetown rice plantations. This book has had five printings, and I always kept a copy of her book on my boat so that I and my guests could refresh our memory of the origin and history of the many plantations we passed on the rivers.

Mrs. Quattlebaum has returned to the plantation after teaching in Charleston and has restored her family home among the beautiful live oaks, which looks out on Waverly Creek and beyond to the river.

13

WACCAMAW RIVER AND MURRELLS INLET BOATS

For me it is a thrill to be on the water in any kind of boat. That's true from the time my father took me at age five on the Fall River Line steamer from New York to Boston up to the time I was in the Navy during World War II and battling a hurricane in the North Atlantic.

My first boat as a six-year-old at the Inlet was a flat-bottomed rowboat, but I soon learned that there was an easier way to make a boat go. I rigged a sail from an old sheet with an oar for a mast and had my first bout with wind and wave. I had caught the sailing bug.

When I was about ten, Henry Buck of Curlew Point bought in New York a beautiful sailing sloop about twenty-five feet long with five sails. While the owner was rigging the boat, I hung around hoping to be invited to sail. I soon became jib monkey on his *Wig Wag*, and you cannot imagine a happier boy.

When my father returned from a buying trip to New York, he would bring me a model of the current America's Cup champion and I knew them all from the *America* to the *Shamrock*. A great thrill recently was when Ted Quantz took Suzanne and me to the New York Yacht Club to see the real America's Cup and the models of all the contenders through the years.

One of the early boats that took people deep-sea fishing at the Inlet, circa *1915.*

My twelfth-birthday present was a sailing canoe, which I named *Scout* for the troop I had joined that year. Henry Mullins also had a sailing canoe at the Inlet, and later Colonel Monroe Johnson bought one and named it *Rainbow* for his famous World War I army division.

The Colonel, who had succeeded General Douglas MacArthur as division commander, owned the cottage just north of Tuck'em Inn. He was a dynamic character and there was no stopping a job begun around the Colonel. Fishing, swimming, or sailing could wait till you finished.

Dr. Julius Mood, owner of the Buckeye cottage, had twin grandsons Preston and Norwood who spent summers at the Inlet with him. For their twelfth birthday, Dr. Mood gave them a sailboat built for them by a local builder. Named the *Surprise,* it was a good sailing sloop with a centerboard and rigged with mainsail and jib.

There was a lot of conversation about whether the *Surprise* was faster than the colonel's *Rainbow.* Finally the colonel challenged the twins to race to Beach Landing and back for the championship of Sunnyside and Murrells Inlet. The date was set for high tide on a Saturday. Colonel

Johnson asked me to crew for him and the twins asked Bill Peterkin.

The race day came with a ten- to twenty-knot southwest breeze, and Henry Buck started the race with a gun. The tide was coming in, and both boats had a tacking duel against the wind and tide up Main Creek. It was soon evident that the *Surprise,* which was built for sailing with a centerboard and jib, had an advantage over the *Rainbow* which was lateen-rigged with no jib and no centerboard.

The *Surprise* was about a tenth of a mile ahead when we reached Beach Landing and the turn for home, but the colonel was confident that he could catch up on the homeward stretch with the wind on his stern and no tacking to do. The lead was too great. Although we overcame some of it, the *Surprise* sailed into Sunnyside Creek by the finish marker several boat lengths ahead.

The colonel soon after left the Inlet, either because he had lost his sailing superiority or because he had been appointed to the Interstate Commerce Commission in Washington.

There's a story about another memorable boat race. Henry Buck and J.D. Murchison had heard the creek boys bragging about who was the best oarsman, so they got up a purse and set a date for a rowboat race from Curlew Point to Beach Landing near the mouth of the Inlet. Much preparation was made. The boats were taken out of the water, the bottoms were sanded and painted, and some even waxed to make them go faster.

A good crowd gathered and Mr. Buck started the race with a gun, and Mr. Murchison was stationed at the mouth of Whale Creek to see that the racers followed the course.

The racers had a choice of going by the main channel or going through Whale Creek. There were about twenty boats entered and lots of splashing and yelling when the race started. Some finished and some did not, but Richard Knox won the race and was presented the prize. He was for many years considered the best oarsman at the Inlet.

The Comanche, *last of the river boats to make scheduled runs from Conway to Georgetown, was the only steamer to use the new screw propeller. She made her last run in 1920.*

In those days we used to go over to Wachesaw to see the riverboats dock and unload their passengers and freight. Large crowds of whites and blacks waited at the landing to meet the boat and hear the whistle blow and the stevedores chant.

There was Captain Thompson on the *Burroughs* and Captain Sarvis on the *Comanche*. Although Captain Sarvis had only one arm, he could wrap his stump around the steering wheel and bring her to the dock without disturbing a piling. As the only means of public transportation for the whole of the Waccamaw Neck, the steamers carried passengers and freight three times a week from Conway to Georgetown. They left at six o'clock in the morning with stops at Toddsville, Bucksville, Enterprise, Bucksport, Longwood, Wachesaw, Laurel Hill, Brookgreen, Sandy Island, Waverly Mills, Hagley, and Georgetown.

The first outboard motor owned by our family was a Caille. You started it with a hot-shot battery and then switched it over to the magneto, much like the Model T Ford. A neighbor had an early Evinrude, and I remember the hours he spent cranking and working on his motor to make it run.

By spring of 1937 I had a bad case of boat fever. The

Bachelor had been sold in the course of my change in marital status, but Tuck'em Inn just needed a sailboat.

The skipper talked the mate out of a dining-room rug, which we needed, and we ordered a snipe-class sloop. The snipe, designed a few years before, had become very popular. She was a good sailor, did not draw much water, and had a kick-up centerboard and rudder so we could maneuver her over the oyster rocks and sandbars.

Christened the *Suzie Q*, she was the only sailboat on the Inlet at that time. We often attached the outboard, ran out to the mouth of the Inlet, fished awhile, then sailed home. Of the many people who enjoyed sailing the boat, Sam Norwood, who became a doctor in Atlanta, was so enamoured of the class that he was elected commodore of the International Snipe Sailing Association in Tokyo in 1962.

In 1939 another Suzie Q came to Tuck'em Inn, weighing about seven pounds, with brown eyes. Soon she learned to say, "Daddy, let's go sailing." Suzie became a good sailor and in her college years was an instructor at Camp Green Cove on Lake Summit near Hendersonville, North Carolina.

Also in 1939, C.T. Sloan, Cy's father, purchased a new boat to be delivered to him in Newport News, Virginia. He invited me to help bring the boat down the waterway.

He had employed Wendell Holbert of Conway as boat captain and sent him to Port Clinton, Ohio, while the boat was being built, so he would be familiar with every detail. I suspected Mr. Sloan had been sold a bill of goods, as Wendell was not a captain, but an accountant in Conway.

Anyway, Cy and his father, Billy Barret—whom I assumed was a friend of Cy—and I met the boat in Virginia. Supplies such as dishes, silver, and food were bought from a ship chandler and stowed, along with charts, tide tables, and other cruising needs. The *Spenddrift* was a beautiful yacht with sleeping quarters for eight people in two cabins, an owner's cabin in the stern, and a crew cabin with two bunks and a head in the bow. A large flying bridge with windshield and top was above the main cabin and you could run her

The Suzy Q.

from either the flying bridge or the main cabin if the weather was bad. She was powered by a pair of Kermath marine engines and cruised comfortably at eighteen knots.

The boat dealer in Newport News sent one of his men with us as far as Elizabeth City, North Carolina, to see that everything was shipshape. He climbed up on the flying bridge, took off his shoes and socks, reared back with his bare feet on the wheel, and steered her this way all the way to Elizabeth City.

There are two routes down to Albermarle Sound and we chose the Dismal Swamp Canal route which has locks on both ends. This canal was surveyed by George Washington before the Revolutionary War. It is a pretty black-water canal but there was a speed limit of six miles an hour to keep the wake of the boat from washing the banks. We were eating breakfast just as we were entering the first lock, and the lockkeeper's wife brought us out a pan of hot biscuits to add to our meal.

At Elizabeth City, Mr. Sloan had an attack of some kind and we had to call a doctor. He was allowed to go on if we would carry a nurse. The doctor suggested his office nurse, and she stayed with us all the way home.

On the first day out, I had pitched in to help cook, make up bunks, and wash dishes. The second day Cy called me aside and told me that I could work if I wanted to, but Billy Barrett was a paid steward and employed for this trip.

We stopped at Socastee which was convenient for Mr. Sloan to be checked by his doctor. The man who ran the store near the dock came to see the boat and asked how many cases of Coca-Cola he would have to sell to get a ride on the *Spenddrift*.

I rode home to Marion with Cy and told my wife Suzanne that if I was going to have a boat I didn't want to wait until I was old and sick.

After my trip on Mr. Sloan's new boat, the bug started biting something awful. I wanted a cruiser about thirty feet long with accommodations for four, an open cockpit in the stern with the motor under the floor, and a reliable marine engine with two-to-one reduction gear.

I looked at used boats from Baltimore to Jacksonville, most often accompanied by my friend and boating companion Bill Hall. Upon finding nothing to my liking, I contacted several boat builders including the Mt. Pleasant Boat Company on Shem Creek in Mt. Pleasant and, in North Carolina a boatyard on the sound behind Wrightsville Beach, the Solomon Brothers of Harkers Island above Beaufort, and the Barbour Boat Works in New Bern.

An interesting story on Harkers Island is that almost all the residents had once lived on the Outer Banks near Cape Lookout. So many storms and hurricanes damaged them that they decided that they would all tear down their houses piece by piece, take them by sailboat to Harkers Island which was more protected, and re-erect them. Many of the families are still there fishing, crabbing, and building boats, as did their fathers and grandfathers before them.

The writer found his love at the Barbour Boat Works, which had just completed a boat for the Walter Stilleys of Conway named *Br'er Rabbit*. We agreed on a price and size. She was to be twenty-eight feet long, lap-strake planked with juniper, and have a Grey marine engine with the desired reduction gear.

The yard's custom was to assign one man as foreman for each boat. He could call on help, but it was his boat until it was finished and launched. We drew Captain Bill Thurston. He never worked without a big chew of tobacco in one cheek and usually a bottle of beer in one hand. He was a master craftsman, raised on the Outer Banks with the Old English accent. Captain Bill could not draw a straight line or read a set of plans, but he could squint one eye, look at a board, and go and cut a piece to fit it perfectly. He really built us a fine boat.

We made many trips to New Bern while the boat was being built, often taking the Pat Treadways or some other couple from Marion with us. We would stop by Orton Plantation outside Wilmington to see the gardens or visit Brunswick Town on the Cape Fear River, one of the early capitals of North Carolina which was destroyed by the British.

Between Wilmington and Jacksonville, we would pass through the little fishing village of Hampstead, the spot capital of the world which celebrated the fish each fall with a festival, dances, watermelon parties, and election of a Queen of Spots. Farther north was Holly Ridge where the army was building Camp Davis as war clouds were gathering. Fighting had already started in Europe, and Uncle Sam was hustling to get us in better military shape. Beyond Camp Davis, Jacksonville was changing from a small fishing village to a small city as the marine base at Camp Lejeune grew rapidly and Cherry Point became a large base. When we spent the night in New Bern, we usually stayed at the Old

WACCAMAW LINE OF

STEAMERS

RATES OF  FREIGHT,

Including Wharfage, Shipping,

From Georgetown to Conway and all Landings

ON

THE WACCAMAW RIVER.

PACKAGES.	FREIGHT.
Barrels Sugar	10
Barrels Flour, Lime, Cement, Plasters, fertilizers, Apples, Onions, Potatoes, Fruit, and all other light and dry barrels each	25
Barrels Liquor, Molasses and all other wet or heavy barrels, each	50
Barrels, empty, each	10
Bags Coffee, Spices, &c., each	25
Bags Flour, each	15
Bags Guano, each	25
Bags Shot, each	05
Bales Domestics	50
Bales Hay, each	30
Half Bales Hay	20
Bundles Forks, Shovels, Spades, Sieves, Saddle Trees, Snaths, Scythes and Collars (of one dozen each	30
Bundles Spokes, Felloes, Shafts, Hubs	25
Bundles Cotton Ties	10
Bundles Hoop Iron	10
Boxes Pianos, Oil Cloth and Machinery	06 pr ft.
Boxes Dry Goods, Saddlery, and other similar boxes	06 pr ft.
Boxes Hats and Shoes	06 pr ft.
Boxes Oranges, Lemons, &c	25
Boxes Axes	25
Boxes Soap, Candles, Pipes, Raisins, Cheese, each	15
Boxes Tobacco	25
Boxes Bacon	60
Boxes Cordials, Syrup, Wine, Liquors, Oils, and all other small boxes not otherwise enumerated	20@25
Boxes Herrings, each	5
Bundles Buckets, Brooms, and Tubs	25
Bagging, in pieces 30 yds., per piece	25
Bagging, in rolls of 100 yds., per roll	50
Bagging, in rolls of 50 yds., per roll	25
Buggies	3 00
Carriages on four wheels, each	4 00 @ 5 00
Chairs, sitting, each	10@20
Coal, per ton, in hhds	2 00

PACKAGES.	FREIGHT.
Corn, per bushel	5
Crates of Crockery	06 per ft.
Corn Shellers, each	50
Cans Oil, each	25@50
Cotton Gins, per saw	06
Cows, each	3 00
Calves, each	1 00
Casks Crockery and Hardware	1 00 @ 2 00
Casks Porter, Ale, in Bottles	60
Demijohns, full, each	25@50
Fertilizers, in Bags, per 2,000 lbs	2 00
Furniture	Per Agreement.
Grindstones, each	25@40
Hhds. Bacon, per 100 lbs	12
Hollow Ware of all kinds, per piece	3@4
Hay Cutters, each	50
Horses, Mules and Asses, each	3 00
Half Bbls. Molasses, Liquor, and all other wet or heavy half bbls. each	30
Iron and other Metals, per 100 lbs	20
Kegs Powder	50@75
Kegs Butter, Nails, Spikes, Shot, (100 lbs.) Copperas, Soda, &c	25
Kegs Paint, each	15@40
Kits Fish, &c., each	15
Lumber of all kinds, reduced to board measure, per thousand feet	Per Agreement.
Laths for Plastering, per thousand	1 00
Mattresses, each	50@75
Mats Bacon, per 100 pounds	20
Oats, per Bushel	05
Paper, Wrapping, per ream	05
Ploughs, Cultivators, &c., each	25@50
Salt, per sack	25
Stoves and Grates	06 per ft.
Tierces of Lard	60
Trunks, Clothing, Shoes, &c	06 per ft
Tubs Butter and Lard	25
Wheelbarrows, each	25
Willow Wagons and Children's Carriages	60
Wagons	3 00 @ 4 00

All articles not enumerated, to be charged for in proportion to above rates.

B. A. MUNNERLYN, Agt. Georgetown, So. Ca.

D. T. McNEILL, Ag't. Conway, So. Ca.

JANUARY, 1885.

Rates of freight for the Waccamaw Line of steamers.

The Mitchelle C, *one of the steamboats of the Waccamaw Line.*

Gaston Hotel, which was over a hundred years old and full of antiques and atmosphere.

Captain Bill and the Barbour Boat Works made good progress on the boat and told us she would be ready to launch in April of 1940. We had a formal christening, and as you can guess, she was named the *Suzanne*. While planning to bring her down from New Bern, we bought dishes and sheets and even curtains for windows or portholes. My first mate could not make the trip due to baby troubles, so Dad and Muz agreed to go.

We purchased charts of the Intracoastal Waterway but could find no chart for the Neuse River which we would run from New Bern to its intersection with the waterway at Adams Creek. We asked some old fishermen about charts, and they told us all we had to do was stay between the net stakes until we reached the waterway. This worked fine because it was shad season, and fisherman had stakes for their nets toward the middle of the river on both sides.

The trip was beautiful, and we had no trouble except our new galley stove was temperamental. We passed Morehead City, traveled down beautiful Bogue Sound, and docked at Swansboro for the night. Dinner on board was good, thanks

The Gov. Safford, *another Waccamaw River steamboat, cruising north.*

to Muz and a few unkind remarks about the alcohol stove. She elected to sleep in the bottom bunk, I had the top bunk, and Dad had the honeymoon suite, a double bed made by folding down the dinette. A rain squall about two o'clock sent me out to check the lines. The next morning Muz reminded me that when I held my feet over the side of the bunk to brush off sand, it went in her face.

We cruised down Masonboro Sound and through Topsail Sound, stopping behind Wrightsville Beach for gas. We took the cut behind Carolina Beach into the Cape Fear River and tied up at Southport, a quaint fishing town, for another night. The morning run by Shallotte to Little River was uneventful but pretty. We turned at Little River and proceeded down the waterway through the canal behind Myrtle Beach. The bridge at Socastee was slow to open, but we gave it a wave and headed for Bucksport. The run down the Waccamaw River was beautiful and the crew all agreed that this was the prettiest part of the trip.

14

THE BUCKS

There was an old house at Murrells Inlet at Bucks Landing, and when we were small we called it the haunted house. We were reluctant to walk by at night, imagining ghosts and pirates coming out of every room. Duneen was built by Captain Henry Buck who came to the area in 1828 and established two lumber mills on the Waccamaw River: Bucksport known as the lower mill and Bucksville known as the upper or middle mill. Henry Buck was energetic and prospered by selling his lumber in New England and the West Indies. A prominent rice plantation owner wrote about always having fresh fruit purchased from West Indian ships on the way to Bucksport or Bucksville with merchandise to be traded for lumber, shingles, and naval stores.

Another story on Captain Buck was that he established the first ice business in Horry County. The sailing ships that came into Bucksport from New England in the winter to load lumber for northern markets would carry ice for ballast, and Captain Buck would sell this ice to the local people for ice cream and other delights.

Prior to the War Between the States, Henry Buck purchased Woodburn plantation from J. Motte Alston and became a rice planter as well as a trader. The house on the coast at Bucks Landing was occupied by the Buck family in the summer.

Tombstone of Jonathan Buck, the founder of Bucksport, Maine, showing the crack on the stone in the shape of a woman's leg.

Captain Henry was a great grandson of Jonathan Buck who settled Bucksport, Maine. The men were good choosers of town sites, for there are no prettier locations in the world than Bucksport on the Penobscot River and Bucksport on the Waccamaw. Both black-water rivers are very beautiful.

There is a Maine story that Jonathan Buck was elected magistrate and in the early seventeen hundreds he tried and sentenced a local woman for witchcraft and had her whipped. She put a curse on Judge Buck and swore that an outline of her leg and the whip marks would show up on his grave. Sure enough, the marks on her leg can be seen on his tombstone.

W.L. Buck took over operation of the mills on the Waccamaw River after the death of his father Captain Henry. In 1874 he decided he would try the shipbuilding business. Instead of shipping his lumber and naval stores to the builders in New England, he would bring the builders to his mill at Bucksville. He was very ambitious in wanting to construct full-scale clipper ships such as the ones that had recently helped America wrest shipping supremacy from the British.

He hired Captain Jonathan Nichols and Master Builder Elishua Dunbar from Eastport, Maine, along with one hundred and fifteen ship carpenters, joiners, and riggers. In September a keel was laid, and a ship was launched in May of 1875. Named *Henrietta* for the daughter of Captain Nichols, she measured two hundred and one feet long with a beam of forty-five feet. She was square rigged as were most of the larger sailing ships at that time.

After she was launched they found that she drew thirteen feet of water—a real problem since the depth of water over the bar at the mouth of Winyah Bay was only twelve feet at high tide. But Yankee ingenuity and Southern know-how came up with an idea to construct a cradle to go under the ship. They fastened two hundred turpentine barrels to the cradle and filled the barrels with water to submerge the cradle and get it under the ship. When this was done, they pumped the water from the barrels, and the added buoyancy lifted the ship enough to clear the bar. The *Henrietta* was afloat in the Atlantic. The tug which took her down the river towed the unharmed cradle and barrels back to Bucksville.

During her tow down the river, crowds of people at every

landing waved and cheered the largest ship ever built on the Waccamaw River and probably the largest ever built in South Carolina. Two other ships—the *Henry Buck,* a barque-rigged sailing vessel, and a schooner named *Hattie Buck*—were built in Bucksville.

The *Henrietta* never returned to Bucksville or the Waccamaw country because of the shallow water. After leaving Winyah Bay she sailed north to Maine and Canada where she was loaded for Liverpool, England.

She made several record-breaking trips around Cape Horn to the Orient, bringing back tea and other cargo to Boston and New York. In 1880 she was caught in a typhoon and destroyed near Kobe, Japan.

The cost of the ship fully rigged was about ninety-thousand dollars, three-fourths that of a similar ship built in northern yards. Fearing they would lose business to southern yards, the New Englanders warned Buck that if he continued to build ships, they would purchase no more lumber or naval stores from his company. As most of his trade was with northern markets, the Yankees, as usual, won.

One of the outstanding events at Murrells Inlet before the turn of the century was the marriage in 1896 of Iola Buck to Frank Augustus Burroughs of Conway, member of another prominent Waccamaw family whose steamship line operated between Conway and Georgetown.

It was their steamship *Ruth* that had the honor of bringing the Burroughs family and friends from Conway to Bucks Landing for the grandest social occasion since George Washington's visit on his southern tour after the Revolutionary War—the marriage of Iola and Frank. Young Frank was the steamboat's new captain. After the ceremony and feasting at Duneen was over the bride and groom had to take all of the Burroughs relatives and friends back to Conway before they could have the boat to themselves. They also had to keep the fireman and engineer along to tie up for the night. When the *Ruth*, with the wedding party and

The Henrietta, *built by shipwrights from Maine at the yards of the W.L. Buck Lumber Company, Bucksville.*

The barque Henry Buck, *built at Bucksville on the Waccamaw River.*

guests aboard, passed the Buck mills at Bucksport and Bucksville, the steam whistles were tied down, and the salute was heard for miles up and down the river.

Captain Henry Buck's granddaughter Eugenia Buck Cutts has a cottage now at Bucks Landing, and the Don Richardsons have recently remodeled the "haunted house." Henry Buck III acquired property at Curlew Point now owned by the Quantz family from Timmonsville.

Iola's sister Hattie married a rice planter and owner of the Mt. Gilead farm, which Buck Norwood, grandson of Captain Henry, has developed and made one of the showplaces of the Inlet.

15

THE BURROUGHSES AND MYRTLE BEACH

It was a fortunate day for Horry County and Waccamaw country when Frank Gorham Burroughs was sent from North Carolina to present-day Conway by his father to deliver some naval stores to a business associate. This was just before the War Between the States. Frank liked the pretty little town of Conwayboro on the Waccamaw River and decided to remain there.

The war started soon after, and he enlisted in a local company, the Brooks Rifle Guards, which was being organized for coastal defense. This company later joined with the Tenth Regiment of South Carolina Volunteers, and they were sent to serve in the western theater under Confederate commanders Albert Sidney Johnston, Braxton Bragg, and Joe Johnston.

Burroughs was captured by the Yankees at the battle of Nashville on December 15, 1864, and spent the remainder of the war in their prison near Chicago. When the prisoners were released at the end of the war, a group was sent by rail to Greensboro, North Carolina, to be discharged. The men were in poor physical condition from lack of food and warm clothes. The Greensboro Female College, which had been closed during the war, was opened and turned into a hospital, and these soldiers were nursed and doctored back to health or until they were well enough to return home.

Frank decided to return to Conwayboro and go into the naval stores business which was growing and looked promising at the time. Possibly he also remembered a pretty girl he had met there.

He and Adeline Cooper of Cool Springs just north of Conwayboro were married in November of 1866. Of their eleven children, three of the five boys reached manhood, and five of the six girls lived to be young ladies and marry well. The boys, Frank Augustus, Arthur, and Don, attended local schools, and two of them went on to Bingham Military School in Asheville. Four girls were sent to Greensboro Women's College, where their father had been so well treated on his way home from the war. Lucille, the youngest girl, enrolled at the new Converse Women's College which had recently opened in Spartanburg.

The naval stores business grew and prospered for Frank Burroughs, and he added lumber mills, cotton and cotton gins, and fertilizer and mercantile stores to his enterprises. His first store, called the Gully Store, was opened in Conwayboro. Other stores were opened at Cool Springs, Grahamville, Bayboro, Pine Island, and Port Harrelson on Bull Creek.

Around 1870 Frank joined with B.G. Collins to form Burroughs Collins Company, which is still in existence, although Collins left the firm about 1900.

F.G. Burroughs was not only a far-sighted businessman but also a good citizen and benefactor. In 1880 he gave the land and erected a school building for the education of the children in the community. Known as the Burroughs School, it was transferred to Horry County when public schools began.

The Burroughses, with large business holdings, saw the need for river transportation to supply their stores and farms with fertilizer and merchandise and to get their lumber and naval stores to market. In 1880 they began the Waccamaw line of steamboats with regular passenger and freight services from Conway to Georgetown and points in between.

The F.G. Burroughs, *flagship of the Waccamaw Line,* circa *1915.*

Incorporators were Franklin G. Burroughs, B.G. Collins, H.T. Williams, D.T. McNeil, and Frank Augustus Burroughs.

Their first boat, a steam-powered side-wheeler, was purchased in Wilmington, North Carolina. Named the *Juniper*, the hundred footer had probably been used on the Fayetteville-Wilmington-Southport run on the Cape Fear River. Next came a new boat 150 feet in length and named for the elder Burroughs. Then came shallow-drafted boats like the *Ruth,* which could go farther up the river and into creeks the larger boats could not manage.

The steamboats stopped at regular landings and even at a plantation if there were freight, mail, or passengers to go to Conway or Georgetown. The plantation owner would signal with a white flag to intercept the boat. Captain Ike Williamson of the *Burroughs* tells about a small boat waving a flag to stop him. When he asked what they wanted, the answer was, "Mama say tell sister Rachael to tell Bubba John to come Sunday not Saturday as we goes to town Saturday."

Captain Sarvis of the *Comanche* tells another story about a small boat waving him down near Laurel Hill plantation. When he asked what he could do for them, the answer came back, "Tell Doctor Wardie no use now to send Granny Sister Pyatt to Mamie's as the baby done come."

The *Ruth* was later sold to George Holliday and was operated on the Waccamaw and Little Pee Dee rivers as far up as his stores at Galivants Ferry and Jordanville. After a few years on this route, she was run ashore just south of the bridge at Galivants Ferry and later burned in a forest fire. An old-timer from Columbus County, North Carolina, remembers the *Ruth* in the early 1900s making regular and frequent runs from and to the landings of Pireway and Old Dock on the Waccamaw just south of the lake by the same name. The steamship company was dissolved and the charter surrendered in 1919, about the same time the first bridge was built across the Waccamaw River in Conway.

The Burroughs family continued to purchase land along the coast and on Waccamaw Neck, and their businesses grew and prospered. The three sons of Frank G. joined their father in the Burroughs Collins Company and continued after his death.

A part of the land they purchased around 1900 for the turpentine and lumber business was several thousand acres of sand and bushes which is now Myrtle Beach. The first summer residents at the beach were all Burroughs relatives or business associates from Conway. Since the area had no name, they called a family meeting for suggestions. Mother Burroughs (Adeline Cooper) said, "Why not Myrtle Beach for the number of wax myrtles growing on the property?" This name was chosen.

In 1899 the Burroughs men saw a need for a railroad to bring visitors to their new beach and applied for a charter

Waccamaw Line steamboats, the F.G. Burroughs *and the* Ruth, *loading at one of the Buck mills at Bucksport,* circa *1912.*

for the Conway and Seashore Railroad to run from Conway to Myrtle Beach. The incorporators were B.G. Collins, F.A. Burroughs, A.M. Burroughs, and D.T. McNeil.

This charter was amended in 1903 and the name was changed to the Conway, Coast and Western Railroad with plans for lines to Bucksville and Bucksport on the river and north along the coast to Southport, North Carolina, joining with the Atlantic Coast Line in Marion. The railroad, completed to Myrtle Beach and as far west as Cool Springs, was then sold to James Chadbourn, who changed the route to go through Loris and Tabor City, joining the Atlantic Coast Line at Elrod near Chadbourn, North Carolina.

I didn't know F.G. Burroughs, but I remember his three sons as active and versatile men. I imagine when the first run of the railroad was made to Myrtle Beach, it was a gala event with half of Horry County in attendance and the Burroughs boys in full charge with Frank as the conductor, Arthur as engineer, and Don out on the cowcatcher waving his ten-gallon hat.

The Burroughs sons envisioned Myrtle Beach as a popular resort, so in 1901 they contracted to have a modern hotel built. Named the Seaside Inn, it was located facing north just east of where US 17 Business intersects Highway 501. They announced in the local papers the hotel's opening and advertised rates of two dollars a day for room and board with discounts for reservations of a week or longer.

Frank A. Burroughs and his wife Iola were the first proprietors. They again advertised in 1906 when the rates had increased to three dollars a day and Hal Buck was manager. Hal was married to Ella Burroughs, a daughter of F.G. and sister of Frank A.

One of the Burroughses tells the story that shortly after the railroad was completed from Conway to Myrtle Beach, a large whale washed ashore at Hurl Rocks Beach just below Myrtle, and the railroad company began running excursions from Conway to the beach to see the whale.

Business was so good that they did not have enough passenger cars to take care of the crowd. They rigged a flat car with chairs to handle the overflow, and the ladies all took umbrellas and parasols to protect them from the sun. Since the engine, *Black Maria,* burned wood, hot ashes rained down on the car throughout the trip. There were "holy" umbrellas and parasols in Conway and Horry County for a long time.

The bones of the whale were later moved to the front yard of the Seaside Inn. I wonder if there wasn't quite an odor near Hurl Rocks Beach between the time the whale washed ashore and the bones were moved to in front of the hotel.

In the early days there were two sections of the Myrtle Beach summer colony. The first houses were covered with hand-drawn cypress shingles on both roofs and walls. Some were painted grey, and others left to weather.

The northern section had cottages belonging to Frank and Iola Burroughs and their sons Edwin and Henry, the Jim Bryans who were connected with the Burroughs Collins Company for a number of years, and the Don Richardsons. Mrs. Richardson was Iola's sister, Jessica Buck, fondly known to her friends and family as Precious.

In the lower section near the present-day pavilion were cottages belonging to the A.W. Barretts, the L.D. McGraths,

Seaside Inn, first hotel in Myrtle Beach.

the George Officers, Dr. Charles Epps, and the Will Freemans, all of Conway, and a cottage owned by Will Townsend of Red Springs, North Carolina. Townsend's company had bought timber rights on land from what is now the airbase down through present-day Surfside Beach and on to Garden City Beach.

Along with W.E. Sikes and R.T. Moore, Townsend built a sawmill for the timber and employed C.A. Roach from Columbia to run it. Roach saw potential in the beach area here, and after they had cut the timber, arranged to buy the acreage which is now Surfside. He had it surveyed and divided into residential and commercial lots and planned a big auction sale for the fall of 1923 when the farmers in the nearby counties had sold their tobacco and had extra money. He named the property Roach's Beach. A storm came through on the Saturday of the sale, and potential buyers failed to appear. Pressed for money to pay his creditors, Roach sold out.

Summer people traveled by car to the beaches the same way we went to the Inlet: down the Georgetown road by Bucksville and across the Waccamaw at Peachtree Ferry and

Maggie, *another of the Waccamaw Line of steamboats, loading freight from a Clyde Line steamer in Georgetown about 1900 for delivery up the Waccamaw River.*

across Socastee Creek by bridge; from there they would bear left to Myrtle and we would bear right to the Inlet.

There was a winding sandy road from Murrells Inlet to Myrtle Beach and continuing on to Little River. It went out on the beach near Windy Hill and Ocean Drive, and you could only cross Singleton's Swash at low tide. Known as the Kings Highway, the road was beautiful with almost a curtain of live oaks and dogwoods on either side with a sprinkling of swamp palmetto and, of course, the wax or sweet myrtle for which the beach was named.

In the late twenties Myrtle Beach was beginning to grow. A newly organized Yacht Club attracted good membership, and they built an imposing building with fishing pier. Their dining room was open to the public. J.D. Murchison, the managing director of the club, became so interested and involved that he sold his house at the Inlet to Jim Carmichael of Bennettsville.

The next generation of the Burroughs family were Edwin, Henry, and Don, Jr., and I often ran into them on the Waccamaw River at Bucksport or Wachesaw. Not long ago I saw this peculiar-looking boat coming down the river with a man in a big hat at the wheel. It turned out to be Don Burroughs, Jr., in a Chinese junk which his son had bought while serving in Vietnam.

16

FIRES AND HURRICANES

The summer of 1918 was memorable. There was a submarine scare along our coast as German U-Boats were sinking our freighters and transports. Many sharks had also been seen, and it was believed that the sinking and loss of life had caused sharks to develop a taste for human flesh. As a result, the summer residents at Sunnyside had built a wire fence in the water around the swimming area at Curlew Point to protect the bathers.

Strolling in front of the cottages, you would see women and children knitting sweaters and scarfs or rolling bandages to be sent to the boys overseas. Children were allowed to knit something simple like a scarf.

The big event that summer was the fire. One afternoon we were on the front porch of Tuck'em Inn mending a net when someone yelled fire. We saw smoke and flames coming through the roof of the Mullins cottage four doors southwest of us. The entire two-story house was engulfed in flames too hot and dangerous to try to get anything out. The wind was blowing hard from the southwest and the heat from the Mullins house soon had the Murchison house next door burning too. As the houses had wood-shingle roofs, they were cracking and sending sparks in our direction.

There was no fire department, and the only water was in the Murchison's wooden tank which soon caught fire and burned. This left us with only a hand pump on the back porch of the Hughes cottage. We formed a bucket brigade and the men spelled each other at the pump. The roofs of the three houses downwind from the fire were wet down.

Help came from neighboring houses and farms, and another crew was formed to beat out the burning shingles that fell on the roofs of Sea Pines, Kamp Kil-Kare, and Tuck'em Inn.

We had moved our furniture out and, as it was low tide, put most of it on the beach along with our automobile. My brother Jack was four years old and he was told to stay in the car until someone came for him.

It looked as if we would surely lose the three houses, when the wind shifted to the southeast. The servant's house and garage back of Sea Pines were all that were destroyed.

We had all given a sigh of relief when we heard someone yelling from the beach. Jack was trying to tell us that the water was coming up around the wheels of the car and the furniture.

Everyone pitched in to push the car out of the water and move the furniture back into the house.

The Mullinses and Murchisons had lost everything, but they were taken in by the other residents and enough clothes were found to help out. The only thing I remember being saved from the two houses was a barrel of beer, which was distributed among the fire fighters. Beer in bottles was packed in wooden barrels with straw to keep the bottles from breaking.

The houses were rebuilt and ready for occupancy by the next summer.

Storms and hurricanes were a major topic of conversation at the Inlet in the early part of the century. Stories were told and retold of the terrible hurricane of 1893 which swept up our coast in August and destroyed beach property from Savannah to Wilmington. Obliterated was a large summer colony with over a hundred houses and a church on North Island where Colonel Peter Horry spent his last sum-

Dr. Ward Flagg, whose family was drowned on Magnolia Beach in the hurricane of 1893.

mers. Another settlement on Debordieu Beach where Joseph Alston and his wife Theodosia Burr summered was washed away.

We were told the story of the Flagg families on Magnolia Beach, now the northern end of Huntington State Park. The house occupied by Dr. Ward Flagg was completely destroyed and he was washed into a tree to which he clung until the storm was over. His bride of a few months was washed from his arms and drowned.

There was no record of the wind velocity in this storm, but the water came high enough to wash away or off of their blocks all of the waterfront cottages at the Inlet.

The next storm to hit the Inlet was in 1908. I was told in both this and a 1916 storm, the Big and Little Pee Dee rivers met in Brittons Neck south of Marion and all transportation was cut off between Marion and Florence.

We were at the Inlet during the 1916 storm, and this was before we had hurricane warnings. The wind began blowing hard from the northeast about the sixteenth of July and continued to increase in velocity for several days. We watched the ocean cover the beach and watched the young marsh chickens float in from their nests on rafts of marsh grass. By Friday night the water was over the bottom step in front of the house, and everyone went to bed that night with their clothes on.

Henry Mullins came by several times during the night to see how we were getting along. At two o'clock in the morning with the wind stronger and water coming in over the floor, it was decided to leave the cottage and go to the pre-Civil War Sunnyside house to wait out the storm.

Sim Goeback, who worked for us at this time, carried Jack and me through the back yard which was three-feet deep in water. It was pouring rain and the wind was blowing around sixty miles an hour, but we reached the Smith's house at Sunnyside safely and found it full with people from all of the cottages.

Some slept, but almost everybody sat on the floor and talked about the storm. Early the next morning the wind had abated, the water was lower, and we felt it safe to go back to the cottage.

The yard was a mess with fallen limbs and trash from the water, but the house was little damaged except for some wet rugs and a few shingles off the roof. As we were still using kerosene lamps, there was no problem of being without electricity. We were soon dried out and back to normal.

The next bad storm to hit the Inlet was Hazel which came in October of 1954 and was much worse than the 1908 or 1916 storms. Beach Landing and Flagg Landing had become

Garden City by this time and there were over a hundred houses on the beach in this area.

We were warned in Marion about the approaching storm by newspaper and radio, but we didn't have time to get to the Inlet and secure the house. The Bigbys from Hartsville were on their way home from the Inlet but had to stop and stay with us in Marion because of the high wind and the falling trees and wires. We listened to the reports on the radio and knew it was a bad blow.

The day after the storm Pratt, Jr., and I started to the Inlet by way of Bucksport to check on the boat. We found the *Suzanne II* in good shape and went on. The road from Conway was covered with limbs, and fallen trees had been removed by the highway department. The National Guard had men stationed at all roads into the Inlet and Garden City to stop the looting. We drove in to the back of the house, and I gave Pratt, Jr., the key to the front door. He came running back to tell me that we didn't need a key because there was no door. It had been smashed in by the wind and water.

There was trash all over the yard, mud and trash in the house; all the front doors were gone and the windows broken. The tide water had been up to the mantel, five feet above the floor. All beds, chairs, and other furniture looked as if someone had put it all in a giant washing machine and turned on the switch. Looking towards Garden City we could see no houses standing, and we counted forty-two houses strewn in the marsh between the inlet and the beach.

We had four small boats in the open garage behind the house and they were all gone. Later we found two of them on the beach about a mile north of the cottage and the other two in the marsh two miles south. The sailboat was a total loss but the others could be patched up and used.

This was just a sample of the damage done by the storm up and down the coast from Georgetown to Southport.

Tuck'em Inn was still on her foundation and we gradually got her in shape for the summer of 1955. Several amusing things that had happened in the storm made the loss and the work easier to bear.

We had an old electric refrigerator in the house which Muz had used in Marion for six or eight years then taken to the Inlet about 1950. When we entered the house after the hurricane, we found the refrigerator face down in the middle of the living room where it had been under water for several hours. We washed it thoroughly with the hose. As soon as the current was back on, it began to run and is still running thirty-five years later. I thought this so remarkable that I wrote the General Electric Company telling them the story. In about a week a short letter arrived from a company official, who was evidently vice-president of their gloom department. He said that he knew they made a good refrigerator, but they really did not intend them to be run under salt water.

Another incident gave us a laugh. After the storm our yard was covered with playing cards and poker chips washed out of all the near cottages. Muz was so afraid that our good contractor Mr. Douglas Brown was going to see them, she made us fall to and pick up every card and chip before he arrived. Mr. Brown, in addition to being a contractor, was a local preacher on Sunday. Muz was sure he would think iniquity had caused the storm.

17

CAMPING AT THE INLET AND BEACH

For more than a hundred years the Inlet has been a favorite spot for campers from the Carolinas. My father told me that they camped at the Inlet before the turn of the century and just after the great hurricane of 1893. Traveling in covered wagons, they camped in the Dozier's front yard (now the Wagon Wheel Farm). He told how they fished with Captain Dozier and that Mrs. Dozier often brought them a pan of hot biscuits to supplement their camp diet.

In the summer of 1922 Colonel Monroe Johnson, who had built a house next to Tuck'em Inn on Rum Gully Swash, invited the Girl Scouts from Marion led by Eloise Bethea to camp at the Inlet and make their headquarters at his cottage, Rainbow Lodge. The troop was the first in Marion and one of the first in the country as the Girl Scout movement had originated in Savannah only a few years earlier. The colonel enlisted Henry Mullins and me with our canoes to ferry the girls over to Goat Island on the ocean for a breakfast cookout. Among this group of girls were Margaret Guerry, Dora Herbert, Hattie Bell Bethea, Lois Sidney Jones, Launa Davis, Lenora Monroe, Frances and Virginia Arters, Helen Hubbard, and Elizabeth McIntyre.

Then there was the time a Marion Boy Scout troop, of which I was a member and Tom Gasque was scoutmaster, was camping in Sunnyside, and some of the boys refused to sleep in the big tent because it belonged to C.L. Pace, an undertaker. On another trip with the Marion scouts, we found a Sumter troop camping nearby. We challenged them to a baseball game and a boxing match with their best boxer against ours. Their boxer was Bill Broughton, and the honor of the Marion troop was defended by Adolph Soloman. I can't remember who won the match, but the cheering was loud.

In 1925 when I entered the University of South Carolina, I made the first organized swimming team there, largely because of my activities in the creeks at the Inlet. As a result, I was offered a summer job as a swimming instructor at Camp Mondamin on Lake Summit between Saluda and Hendersonville, North Carolina. One of the best camps in the mountains, it was owned and operated by Frank Bell, known to all of us as Chief.

Chief conceived the idea of giving each boy at camp a week on the beach. Knowing I was familiar with the Waccamaw area, he appointed me director of the new Camp Big Seawater. Here I was, expecting to spend the summer in the mountains and being sent to run a camp on the ocean just north of the Inlet.

We took off forty strong in an old school bus with Camp Big Seawater painted on the sides and traveled all night, arriving at the beach at seven in the morning. The boys all had to have a swim before breakfast, with or without bathing suits, and so began camp.

Chief had had a mess shack and bunk house erected right down on the beach, but being a mountain man, he did not have the buildings screened. There was a combination cook and caretaker by the name of Andy. I am sure he had worked for the Vereens or was related to the Heywards and Sparkmans for he could really cook, serving us fried mullet, grits, and cornbread along with hot pancakes and good homemade cane syrup.

There were no stores nearby, and we sometimes walked

Girl Scout troop from Marion, circa *1919.*

the two miles to Floral Beach (now Surfside), which was just developing, to purchase a cold drink or bar of candy. Each group of boys sent down went deepsea fishing with Captain Morse, and we seined for mullet on the beach, swam, crabbed, and played baseball.

The sun was pretty hot and some of the boys were badly sunburned. With no screens, the mosquitoes took their toll, but all in all the boys had a great time. The sunburn was treated with cold cream and the mosquito bites with peroxide and alcohol. The boys were sent back to Camp Mondamin browner and thinner but with a good taste of the beach.

Camp lasted a month and I was mighty glad to see the old school bus arrive to take the last group of us back to Lake Summit and Mondamin. I arrived in time to hear Hal Kemp and Jan Garber play for dances in nearby Hendersonville where there were girls by the thousands, and they were good dancers, too.

After I inherited the Marion scout troop from Fred Stubbard in 1930, we camped many times between the Hughes cottage and the Murchison's. Fred Cross, who had an eye for a trade, was along on one trip. He brought a bushel of oranges to sell to the boys at a handsome profit. He took his clothes out of his suitcase and filled it with the oranges, kept it locked, and took it with him everywhere. Whether in the boat fishing or at the beach for a swim, he would unlock the suitcase and sell an orange or two as demand arose. Business was brisk for the first day or so, but then it abruptly stopped. The next time Fred opened the suitcase, the oranges were gone and the suitcase was full of oyster shells and rocks. This was a mystery he never fully solved but he had a suspicion or two.

Besides Fred, campers were Horace Tilghman, Joe Gasque, Archie McIntyre, Harbord Johnson, Harry Edwards, William Schofield, George Andrews, and Josh Johnson.

On another trip we hiked to LeGette's Mill Pond for an overnight campout and to fill the requirements for the seven-mile hike. We had made good time and set up camp for the night when one of the boys told me that George Andrews walked in his sleep. Since a Marion boy had drowned several years earlier on just such a camping trip on the river bank, I was concerned. After much head scratching, I decided to tie George's leg to my leg but to leave enough play in the rope that both of us could turn over. Everything was fine until Joe Gasque, the official taster of the cooking tests, became sick in the night, and in going to help, I forgot about the rope and pulled George several feet along the ground.

We had close calls camping with the Boy Scouts, too. We were on the beach once and the temperature stayed a hundred or above the entire week. The boys didn't do anything but lie in the shade and wait until night to go swimming. John Platt had a touch of sunstroke and we put wet blankets on him. At Camp Nixon once, Harbord Johnson and Harry Edwards were wrestling on an upper bunk, and Harbord fell and broke his arm. Fortunately Dr. Schofield came along, made splints from an apple box, and set the arm.

William Schofield from this troop later represented the Marion scouts and the State of South Carolina at the World Boy Scout Jamboree in Belgium. Four other boys became

Eagle scouts, among the first in the Pee Dee area. They were Bob Huckabee, L.D. Lide, John Giles, and E.T. Hughes.

By now you know I have a weakness for boats, islands, and pretty girls, especially those named Suzanne. One of our memorable trips with the scout troop was to an island named Botany Bay that I bought in 1960. Below Charleston on the North Edisto River and the ocean, the island had all the charm of the South Seas with a mile and a half of ocean beach, palm trees, and white sand. Along with the island came two hundred goats. They had a regular path around and through the area, kept the underbrush eaten down, and were interesting to watch even if they left a few ticks and fleas to remember them by.

On this particular trip Roy Lewis and Reaves Gasque were the troop leaders, and during the weekend we had a great time sleeping in sleeping bags and hammocks with the sound of palm fronds rattling in the breeze. We made chowder from clams gathered in the creek and caught some fish, but the boys were more interested in the goats. I said they could have any goat they could catch, tie up, and get home. They spent the entire morning before we left trying to catch goats, and the goats won. Finally Bill Thompson with two other boys caught one but couldn't tie him securely, so they had to settle for taking home ticks and fleas.

When the island was sold in 1966, we had a farewell party, an all-day event with a picnic dinner and Botany Bay punch. Everyone was ferried to the island by Henry Mullins, Horace Tilghman, and Charles Menefee. Each guest received a lei and a straw hat from Suzy and Duncan McIntyre. S.P. and Mary Watson made coffee over a campfire.

Captain Henry Mullins, recently retired from the United States Navy, lost the second ship under his command while he was ferrying me from the island. He managed to sink an eight-foot skiff and put himself and me in the water. Horace Tilghman came to our rescue.

18

INLET BIRDS

Through the years from the porch at Tuck'em Inn we have enjoyed the birds, and we have been fortunate to have shore birds and what we call land birds. The land birds are mostly nuthatches, chickadees, pine siskins, and occasionally a painted bunting; hummingbirds also are regular visitors.

The hummingbirds are attracted to red and once on the porch I was drinking from a red glass, and a hummingbird came up to the glass to share my nectar. In addition to these, we see doves and boat-tailed grackles with their long tails. The males are black and they feed on the ground and on the oyster rocks. The females are a dark brown and are seldom seen with males as if they have some segregation plan.

Shore birds are many and beautiful with the various species of herons topping the list. We see the night herons, the Louisiana herons, the little green herons, the great white herons, the little white herons, and the snowy egrets with their golden feet and beautiful plumage. One of our most interesting shore birds is the oystercatcher with its red bill that usually sits on an oyster bed and steals the meat from the oysters when they open their shells to take in water or spit it out. In the 1920s the gannet, now endangered, was a common bird with the best organization for fishing of any species I have seen. A flock of thirty or forty of them would line up about a foot apart across a creek when the tide was running out and catch anything coming by, fish, shrimp, or squid.

Ospreys are great fishermen that dive in the water, catch a fish in their claws, and fly away to their nests to eat the prey or feed it to their young. One of the great sights is to see an osprey catch a fish, an eagle descend on the osprey making it drop its fish, and the eagle's catching the fish before it hits the water.

The osprey likes to nest in high trees or on top of channel markers, and the brighter they're colored the better they like them. I counted twenty-nine osprey nests on the Waccamaw River between Wachesaw and Georgetown, and over half of them were built on top of the Intracoastal Waterway markers.

Another interesting coastal bird is the wood ibis which belongs to the stork family. They are big birds with a Roman nose and fly by in V-formations, as do geese and ducks.

One morning after I had spent the night across Rum Gully Swash at the Duncan McIntyres, I saw some birds in the road behind the house scratching and clucking like guineas. Upon looking them up in the bird guide, I found they were purple gallinules, which build their nests in a freshwater marsh. Marsh hens and Carolina rails build their nests in salt marshes. Speaking of marsh birds, we have the marsh sparrow and the marsh wren which feed and live exclusively in the salt marshes or in the spartina grass. Frequent visitors to the marshes are the red-winged blackbirds and the marsh hawks.

Before leaving the subject of birds, I want to mention the gulls which sit on the railing of the piers all day and apparently take life easy until something upsets them. There are large herring gulls, bonaparte gulls with their black hoods, and laughing gulls who sound like a bunch of teenage girls when they are disturbed. Another rail sitter is the kingfisher which dives for fish.

We also have terns with their forked tails and the beautiful black skimmer which glides along the top of the water with its mouth open to catch a shrimp or small fish.

Let's not forget the brown pelican, that beautiful, lumbering bird which flies just above the waves. A few years ago they were on the way to becoming extinct, because widespread use of DDT made their egg shells too brittle to hatch. They are on the way back and I had the privilege a few years ago, on a boat trip to the Outer Banks of North Carolina with Zack Smith, Forrest Ramsey, and the late Bill Harrelson, to stop at some of the pelican nesting islands in Pamlico Sound. We saw the baby pelicans just after they were hatched with their featherless bodies and long bills which looked as if they were shaking a finger at you. The mother pelicans were feeding them with small fish and shrimp, and it was a never-to-be-forgotten experience.

If you are still interested in birds and are down Murrells Inlet way late some afternoon just before dark, turn off Highway 17 Bypass towards Socastee, then turn left to Heaven Gate Church, then right to an old pond and peat-moss quarry. You will see the cranes and herons nesting for the night in the green trees. This is just one of life's little extras.

19

RICE PLANTATIONS TODAY

In 1914 when Tuck'em Inn was built, Brookgreen was considered the area's most beautiful rice plantation with its outstanding avenue of live oaks and the old garden.

A hunting club had purchased it with Dr. Julius Mood of Sumter as the principal owner. They had allowed Dr. Ward Flagg to live in his plantation's old kitchen where he doctored the locals and made good scuppernong wine. As children we visited the plantation often and listened to the tales of Dr. Wardie, as his patients called him.

The Flaggs had also owned the Hermitage at the Inlet, the plantation's summer house where Clarke Willcox now lives. They had a catwalk from the Hermitage all the way across the Inlet to what is now Garden City. Starting in front of the summer home, the walk went across the marsh to Main Creek, which was crossed in a rowboat, then picked up across the creek and proceeded to the beach. They erected a small building on the beach, where they could change clothes or take shelter in bad weather. The Flaggs also had a private road from the plantation to their inlet house, and parts of this old road can be seen today.

When Mr. and Mrs. Archer Milton Huntington came to the area on their yacht *Rocinante* and bought Brookgreen, I thought that here was another rich couple who wanted to enjoy the beauty of our old rice plantations and that they would close it to the public. Little did I realize that they would create one of the most outstanding art and nature exhibits in the Southeast.

When they arrived, I hadn't known that Mrs. Huntington was a famous sculptress. Several years later my wife Suzanne and I were invited to dinner at the National Arts Club in New York where we learned that Mrs. Huntington had won a national award for one of her works. Later in San Francisco, on a bus tour of the city, the guide called our attention to sculpture at the gate of the famous Japanese gardens and told us that it was done by the renowned Anna Hyatt Huntington.

Soon after Mr. Huntington purchased Brookgreen he built for the Sandy Island people a new church, a community center, and a small medical clinic. He would send his workboat, *The Brookgreen*, to pick up passengers who wanted to go to Georgetown to shop or attend to business.

The story of Mr. Hungtington can't end without telling about the time the late Tom Stackhouse of Marion and Florence made an appointment with him soon after Brookgreen's purchase to sell him some insurance or an annuity. Mr. Huntington listened attentively to the sales presentation and responded, "Young man, you are a good salesman and have a good company, but I am not at present interested in investing money. I am trying to give some away and leave my possessions where they will most benefit mankind. Furthermore, I own a good part of your insurance company."

Another tale is that when the gardens were opened to the public, the parking and picnic area was close to the alligator pond. After eating lunch, visitors would leave the scraps or throw them to the alligators. The alligators began to like fried chicken, sweet pickle, and pimiento cheese sandwiches, and it wasn't long before they were coming out when visitors started to unpack their lunches. This was so frightening that soon a ten-foot fence was erected around the pool. I don't know if the gators began climbing the fence, but the trustees of the garden later decided to move them to the lake south of the conservatory. That's where they are today.

The Huntingtons were fortunate in obtaining Frank Tarbox as curator, and later his nephew Gurdon L. Tarbox, Jr. Both worked diligently to transform the old rice plantation into a work of art and nature unsurpassed on the Atlantic Coast. Anyone who drives south on US 17 or visits Murrells Inlet or Litchfield and doesn't take a day to visit Brookgreen has missed one of God's little extras.

Just a few miles south of Brookgreen before the Lafayette bridge to Georgetown is the Baruch Marine Experiment Station given by Belle M. Baruch to South Carolina and operated by the University of South Carolina and Clemson University as a marine center and Hobcaw Oceanic Foundation. The Hobcaw Foundation is on property purchased by international financier Bernard Baruch in 1905 consisting of around seventeen-thousand acres and known as Hobcaw Barony.

Hobcaw is an Indian name meaning "between the waters." A barony was a large tract of land usually twelve-thousand acres or more granted to one of our early landgraves. This tract was first granted to Lord Carteret, one of the Lords Proprietor, and later to Landgrave Thomas Smith.

Probably no other plantation on the Atlantic coast entertained more distinguished men: United States Presidents Cleveland and Roosevelt, Winston Churchill, Generals Marshall, Bradley, and Clark, and numerous senators, cabinet officers, and congressmen. There is a story that in 1920, two ranking senators were visiting Baruch for a duck hunt with one of his guides. After the hunt, the guide told the senators that if they were the ones in Washington making laws doing away with liquor, raising taxes, and couldn't hit a duck any better, they should just go home.

It was during this time that Captain Howard Buxton came to the Inlet, married a local girl, and built a home back of

The J.L. Wheelers and guests in front of their house on South Island, circa *1912.*

Tuck'em Inn on Sunnyside Lane. Captain Buck, as we all called him, was boat captain for Bernard Baruch. Raised on the coast of New Jersey, he had built and operated boats all of his life. His main duty at Hobcaw was to make trips to Georgetown for mail and telegrams and meet any guests that might be arriving to visit the Baruchs.

Captain Buck had a well-equipped workshop in back of his house, and he built several boats in his back yard. It was a fascinating place to hang out for a young fellow who loved boats. I learned how to tie knots, splice a rope, and rig a sailboat. Captain Buck also had some good tales to tell.

A few miles from Georgetown you can visit North and South islands given to the state by the late Tom Yawkey as a wildlife refuge. Joe Wheeler, as his friends called him, was a colorful character, and it was he who interested the Yawkeys in North and South islands and in South Carolina.

J.L. Wheeler was a lumberman who came to Marion from Pennsylvania. He operated lumber mills there and in Poston on the Pee Dee River near Johnsonville and had interests in mining in Canada and timber holdings in Pennsylvania and South Carolina. He visited Tuck'em Inn often and would tie up his yacht, the *Tamiskaming,* at Wachesaw and ask J.D. Murchison to check the engines for him. The yacht was named for his silver mine in upper Canada. In 1909 he purchased North and South islands from General Alexander.

Wheeler knew William Yawkey who was also in the lumber business in Michigan and whose family had become very wealthy. He invited Yawkey to South Island to visit and to hunt. At the time Yawkey owned the Detroit baseball team and brought Ty Cobb down with him for the shooting along with his nephew and adopted son Tom. Yawkey fell in love with the island and persuaded Wheeler to sell him a lot across from their lodge. Thereafter the Yawkeys stayed almost all winter.

I visited the islands several times as a boy and went on deer drives and duck hunts with Mr. Wheeler, the Yawkeys, and Ty Cobb. On one hunt we brought in over two hundred ducks and seven deer. It was a memorable event for a ten-year-old boy. My mother told me that I cut my first tooth aboard the *Tamiskaming* on a trip to South Island. Perhaps that is the reason for my enduring love of boats and islands.

After William's death, Tom inherited his father's property in the islands and his love of baseball. Eventually he purchased the Boston Red Sox and brought another famous baseball player to the islands—Ted Williams. Joe Wheeler died in 1932 during the bottom of the Depression, and Mrs. Wheeler sold the balance of both North and South islands to Tom Yawkey. The next time I visited South Island, Jim Gibson was the caretaker and all the boys on the island were wearing Red Sox baseball caps and blazers.

At Tom's death the islands went to the state along with an endowment fund of ten-million dollars to take care of them. All of us in South Carolina should be grateful to Joe Wheeler for introducing the Yawkeys to the good life at the coast, and give thanks that Tom Yawkey appreciated North and South islands and his adopted state.

So here within twenty-five miles one can see and visit three of the outstanding attractions in the eastern United States: Brookgreen, Baruch Marine Experiment Station, and North and South islands, all of which evolved from the area's fabled rice plantations.

20

WATERWAYS AND JAILBIRDS

In the summer of 1933, Frank Salmon, my brother Jack, and I decided that we had explored almost all of the waters nearby and we would do some pioneering with boats driven by outboard motors. Outboard motors had been improved to the extent that they would usually get you where you were going and almost always get you back. We planned to run the Intracoastal Waterway from Wachesaw Landing in back of Murrells Inlet to Charleston in our fifteen-foot Thompson boat powered by a twelve-horsepower Johnson motor.

Since there were no marinas in those days selling gas, we collected six five-gallon cans for extra gas, plus life jackets, oars, oarlocks, lines, and a first-aid kit. We planned to spend the night at Tuck'em Inn and leave early in the morning on July 4. Awake by three o'clock, we reached Wachesaw and were off at daybreak after a rousing send-off by Elizabeth McIntyre and Mary Sale who were staying next door in the Johnson cottage.

We had a good run down the Waccamaw River to Georgetown, but found Winyah Bay pretty rough. As we had no top or windshield, every wave gave us a wetting. The Estherville-Minin Creek Canal was calm, so we dried off and ran behind South Island to the North Santee River without mishap, making good time. Then we picked up more rough water, and the July sun was beginning to bear down.

Before reaching McClellanville we checked our gas and found that we had already used more than half of our supply to come less than half the way to Charleston. Finding no gas stations near the water, we left the boat, each taking a five-gallon can, to walk to the highway over a mile away. Let me tell you, five gallons of gas can get mighty heavy when you are walking.

We were under way again about eleven, having already eaten our lunch and a box of brownies the girls had given us for the trip. At this time the waterway was incomplete, and the route entered Bull's Bay from McClellanville and went through a series of winding creeks past Seewee Bay, Capers Island, and the Isle of Palms. We passed back of Sullivan's Island about four o'clock and had started across Charleston Harbor when the breeze began picking up and blowing a young gale. The waves were tossing us around pretty good and the boat was taking in some water, so we decided to turn around and land behind Sullivan's Island. We arranged with a man to watch the boat overnight, took our clothes which were packed in duffel bags, and caught a bus for Charleston to look for a place to spend the night.

We stopped at the first place that advertised rooms for rent, the old Argyle Hotel on Meeting Street. The clerk looked us over pretty carefully but gave us a room and bath. Did those beds and that tub look good. We put in a call for five o'clock the next morning to make the trip back. Frank decided that he had business to attend to in Charleston and called Wilbur Hook, who was in medical school there, to take him to the bus station later in the day. We left him sleeping—and to pay the bill.

No buses ran at that hour in the morning so we hailed a jitney making its run to Sullivan's Island and squeezed in between two overweight cooks on their way to the island to fix breakfast.

The jitney put us out near the boat and we found

everything in good shape except the gas. Again we hefted the five-gallon cans and found a filling-station about half a mile from the boat. We bought gas and the oil to mix with the gas plus a package of Nabs and a Coke for breakfast, leaving us with only a dollar and seventy-five cents between us and the possibility that we would again need gas at McClellanville.

After a hurried conference, we decided that if worse came to worse we could pawn Frank's watch which he had loaned us for the trip back. The filling-station operator gave us a ride to the boat and we were on our way. We made good time to McClellanville but again used a lot of gas and thought it best to call Dad to meet us at the South Island Ferry, about fifteen miles this side of Georgetown.

We arrived near the expected time, and Dad never looked so good as when we saw him waiting at the ferry slip. We arranged to dock our boat, put our duffel bags in the trunk of the car, and fell asleep before Dad had driven a mile.

That same summer Bob Whittenberg, the younger brother of Mrs. Jim Carmichael who lived next door to Tuck'em Inn, called from Bennettsville and asked me to go to Myrtle Beach with him in Jim Carmichael's new Ford. We would drive down Saturday afternoon, attend the dance that night at the Myrtle Beach pavilion, and go to the Inlet for the night.

Bob picked me up in Marion in Jim's new Ford V-8 equipped with special racing gears, the latest thing in fast cars. He couldn't wait to demonstrate the pickup and speed of the new car and began to step on it when we reached South Main Street. We heard the siren behind us, but Bob paid little attention. When leaving the city limits, we were doing seventy-five or eighty miles per hour and were far ahead of the pursuing car.

We stopped at Galivants Ferry for a Coke, and Bob invited me to drive the new car. We changed seats and proceeded at a more than moderate speed through Aynor. On the outskirts of Conway there was a roadblock with several police cars. Policemen quickly seized me and escorted both of us in no uncertain way to the Conway Police Station. The chief of police examined my driver's license and told us that the Marion police had called on them to stop the car. They suspected we were bootleggers and knew that we had broken the speed limit and outrun the Marion police.

Their instruction was that the driver was to put up a hundred-dollar bond or go to jail. This was a lot of money for two young men who had only wanted to go to a dance at the beach and didn't have but ten dollars between us. The police, finding no liquor in the car, let me call Mr. Barrett at his hardware store. He cashed a check for us and we were on our way.

The dance was boring, the music was poor, and the girls were bad dancers and not even pretty. We thought constantly of the money we had lost. One hundred dollars was a lot of money in 1933—a whole month's salary.

Next morning P.W. Johnson, the mayor of Marion, stopped by Tuck'em Inn after breakfast to tell about the bootleggers who had come through Marion the afternoon before: how they had outrun his police car, how he had phoned Conway to stop and fine them; how he thought they were in the Conway jail.

My head was hanging pretty low, but I told Mr. Johnson that he had arrested two boys headed for a dance at the beach. He was much surprised but told us that if we would go to the police office in Marion on Monday morning, he would have them refund our money.

The sun shone a little brighter on Rum Gully Swash, the memories of the dance became a little better, and some of the girls seemed almost pretty.

By December that year, we were at the bottom of the Great Depression and things were pretty dull around Marion. Our family decided to spend Christmas at Tuck'em Inn. It was also decided that no one was to spend over fifty cents for a present, and all presents were to be put in a trunk and opened at the Inlet on Christmas morning.

Dad and Muz, Aunty Fan, Kakie, and Catherine Sparkman were going to go directly to the Inlet. My brother Jack, Sip, and I planned to go to Georgetown by car and take the *Bachelor,* our cabin cruiser, up the Waccamaw River. Dad would meet us at Brookgreen on Christmas Eve and take us over to the cottage.

We expected to get a little work out of Sip such as cleaning up and polishing brass on the boat, so we could spend Christmas day on the Waccamaw River. But Winyah Bay was a little rough, and Sip found the dead center of the boat and held on for dear life. He did not move or turn loose until we reached the dock at Brookgreen.

Kakie and Aunty Fan had Tuck'em Inn decorated with holly, yaupon, and red candles on the mantel, and they even had a small Christmas tree decorated with seashells. We had our turkey that night and made sandwiches to take on the boat the next day.

The trunk was opened Christmas morning after breakfast, and the presents were passed around. It was surprising what fifty cents would purchase in the way of a present in 1933.

After we took Catherine and Sip to their brother's house on the Wachesaw road to spend the day with their family, we drove on to Brookgreen and the boat. Mrs. Genevieve Willcox Chandler was on duty in the gardens, and we all stopped to exchange greetings with her.

It was a beautiful day and I am sure the Lord was trying to make up for the hard times our country was going through. We cruised out Brookgreen Creek with the leaves falling all around, and the wake of the boat lapping the cypress knees near the bank. On such a pretty day the turtles were out on logs enjoying the sunshine.

We stopped at Sandy Island to wish Prince Washington and his family a Merry Christmas, and he had the island quartet sing a Christmas carol for us. Then we went up river to Bucksport for some gas, saw Don Richardson, and waved at the many children who had come down to the store on the dock.

Our Christmas lunch was eaten as we moved through Prince Creek, and we touched shore at Brookgreen around four o'clock. Sip and Catherine had beaten us back to Tuck'em Inn and had a big fire going in the fireplace and a pot of clam chowder on the wood stove in the kitchen. Everyone agreed that it was one of the best Christmases they had ever spent.

Next day Jack and I took the boat to Georgetown, picked up the car, and drove back to Marion. Sip decided to return by car as that bay was too rough for him.

In the 1920s and '30s there was an annual Fourth of July picnic when the people of Sunnyside would all go and picnic at Beach Landing on present-day Garden City. We would go by boat for an all-day outing with the usual menu of fried chicken, sandwiches, potato salad, pickles, and always watermelons for dessert.

Not everyone summering at the Inlet owned a motorboat or outboard motor but most cottages had a rowboat. On community social events like this we traveled in tandem with motorboats towing the rowboats. Sometimes one powerboat towed four or five rowboats filled with picnickers and fried chicken.

21

THE BACHELOR

In the fall of 1929 I came back to Marion after being away at school for four years and working in the mountains in the summers. Things were pretty quiet. Frank Salmon was working in the Marion National Bank, Pete Bostick was running the ice plant on Railroad Avenue, Bob Jones was operating the Gulf station next to the Old Opera House, and Buster Joyner was teaching and coaching football. Henry Mullins was at the Naval Academy learning to be an admiral, and Paul Barham was in medical school getting information on tonsils.

Business was bad and getting worse, but the tide was still rising and falling on Rum Gully Swash and the moon was shining on Tuck'em Inn. We decided that Murrells Inlet had been neglected, so we propositioned Sip to cook for us and began going down to Tuck'em on weekends.

We usually took dates. Pete took Josephine Hardwick from Mullins. Frank always found the prettiest school-teacher in eastern South Carolina. Bob would take Louise Holliday, and I was usually with some girl the others would pick for me. Hughes Schoolfield would invite Elizabeth McIntyre, and usually Buster and Lucy Joyner would chaperone. Money was scarce, but food was cheap and we could spend the whole weekend for between two and three dollars a couple.

On one weekend during duck season in 1930, Frank and

I were going hunting at daybreak, and Elizabeth McIntyre and Reubie Holliday, scorning our shooting ability, boasted that they would pick and clean all the ducks we killed. Sure enough, we did not bring down a single duck, but on the way back in the boat we shot a couple of fish ducks to bring to the girls. Lib and Reubie did not know that they were not good to eat, so they lived up to their agreement and began picking the ducks on the back porch. We were inside laughing, until Sip, feeling sorry for the girls, told them that they were picking die dappers that were no good. The girls haven't forgiven us yet.

On another trip down to the Inlet that winter, we arrived at Tuck'em Inn after dark. We hustled to get a fire started in the living-room fireplace and in the kitchen as these were our only sources of heat. It was before we had electric lights, and we were gathered around the living-room fire trying to get warm but kept feeling a cold draft on our backs. Upon investigating, we found that some one had broken into the house and had taken out an entire window, glass, frame, sash, and all.

On one of these trips we learned about a cabin cruiser for sale at one of the plantations on the Waccamaw River and decided to investigate. We found a twenty-six-foot Elco for sale at a very reasonable price. She had a four-cylinder Gray marine engine, designed much like the motor in the Model T Ford of our younger days. We had no trouble making it go. There was an open cockpit with deck chairs and, two steps down, the galley with a two-burner alcohol stove and a small sink which also was used for a wash basin. Forward of the galley were upper and lower bunks on either side and the head in the bow. We arranged with the caretaker to meet us on a Sunday and take us out for a trial run. As we started down the river, it began to rain. Frank lowered the cockpit side curtains, and they were full of rats which ran all over us and the boat. Hughes almost went overboard before we finally got things under control.

We liked the boat and our offer was accepted. Since we

Riverfront, Georgetown, circa *1932. The boat at the far left is the* Bachelor.

were unmarried, the boat was renamed the *Bachelor.* We kept her on the river back of the stores in Georgetown, and Bob Oliver, who was captain of the ferry from Georgetown to Hagley, agreed to look after her.

One year in March I planned a trip to Charleston, and as none of the others could get away, I invited Freddie Baker, who still had his neck in a cast from a diving accident. We left Georgetown about ten o'clock on a cold, windy morning and spent the night tied up at the old oyster factory below McClellanville. Next day we were away early. Upon approaching Seewee Bay, we ran on a sandbar where a passing barge had knocked down the waterway marker.

We tried to back off, but she wouldn't budge. Freddie got on the bar and pushed on the bow, but we still stuck fast. I also got off to help, and the boat began to move. We couldn't hold it, so there we were on the sandbar, the boat moving away from us with the wind and tide. We tried to swim for the boat, but each time we almost reached it, a gust of wind carried it farther away.

I finally caught the stern rail, but Freddie was too tired to climb aboard. Then he called that the water was over his head, so I grabbed a rope and went back to him.

We made it to the side of the boat, but we were both so exhausted that we had to spend a long time holding on the boat in the cold water. When we managed to crawl over the stern, we quickly got out of our wet clothes and started the galley stove. Hot coffee and dry clothes sped us on our way to Charleston, and we were tied up at Adger's Wharf before dark.

Since we hadn't had a good meal for several days, we decided to dress in our white linen suits and eat supper at a nearby cafeteria. For dessert Freddie selected the largest cherry tart on display and put it on his tray. On the way to our table another patron bumped him, and the cherry tart jumped to his collar and skittered all the way down the front of his suit leaving a red path. He looked as if someone had cut his throat, and everyone in the cafeteria was laughing so hard they couldn't eat.

Next to the *Bachelor* at Adger's Wharf was a forty-six-foot yacht from New York with a man and his wife aboard. The wife had had enough of boats and was returning to New York by train, so the man asked us to help him take his boat home. He offered to pay all expenses and buy us a ticket back to Charleston.

This offer was too good to refuse and Freddie decided to go, but I had to get back to work in Marion. Next morning both boats headed for Georgetown. As the *Caroline* was a much faster boat, they pulled out of sight as they rounded the Isle of Palms. Freddie returned two weeks later and reported a good trip.

In the summer of 1934 we decided to take the *Bachelor* around to Murrells Inlet and anchor her near the end of the pier at Tuck'em Inn. Captain Buxton agreed to keep an eye on her when we were not there. We did a lot of offshore fishing while she was at the Inlet and took some good trips up and down the coast.

One Sunday several of us took the boat outside to Myrtle Beach and ran in near the shore, stopping just beyond the breakers near the Yacht Club pier. Some of us swam ashore to ask Reubie and Dave Gaston if they wanted to ride back to the Inlet with us in the boat. Frank Salmon and Pete Bostick were keeping her near shore so that they could pick us up when we returned. As we swam out toward the boat, Frank cut the engine speed so we could climb aboard, and the motor cut off. They cranked and cranked and she wouldn't start. Meanwhile wind and waves were pushing us nearer to the beach. It looked as if we were going to pile up on shore, when the old Gray engine coughed a couple of times and started chugging. We were mighty relieved to get away from the surf.

When we were ready to take the boat back to Georgetown, we invited Mrs. James Johnson, her children Prince and Josh, and Edna Miles to make the trip by ocean with us. They all expected to be seasick and began taking medication and sucking lemons a day or two ahead. As we headed out Main Creek, Josh, who was eleven, spied his buddy Frank West fishing with his father. He begged to take the wheel and pass Frank's boat in grand style. I think Frank had been bragging about running a boat to Josh.

No one got sick and we were in Georgetown by early afternoon. Muz met us in the car, and we cleaned up the boat and caught the ferry to Hagley and back to the Inlet. While we were waiting for the ferry, the Georgetown children's quartet sang some spirituals.

By this time Frank and Pete were courting pretty heavy and Hughes was busy with the law, and they wanted to sell their interests in the *Bachelor*. Judge Baker McIntyre and Jake Miles wanted a boat for fishing, so they bought half, and Jack and I kept the other half.

The *Bachelor* spent almost every weekend either fishing near the jetties between North and South islands or cruising Winyah Bay. When we were fishing for bass at the jetties, Jake decided he would lie in the upper bunk and fish with his line out of the porthole. He took a turn of the cord around his ankle to alert him if he had a bite. He was snoring away when something big took his bait and almost pulled Jake through the porthole before we could cut the line.

On one fishing trip we invited Dr. Dibble, our friend and favorite physician, to go along and try his luck. Confined by his practice, the doctor had not fished for a long time, but he landed a thirty-five-pound channel bass. He was so proud of his catch that he spent his fishing time sneaking back to the fish box to peek at his fish.

The next year fishing was not so good, and we decided to sell the boat to Mr. Law in Georgetown for taking out fishing parties. For many years she was a permanent fixture at the dock behind the Georgetown waterfront.

Jack had taken a job away from Marion; I was making frequent trips out of town. Anyway a young man thinking of marriage had no business with a boat named the *Bachelor*.

22

WORLD WAR II

When World War II began, the air force base was established at Myrtle Beach and the whole area was affected by it. Garden City was taken over as a target area for the B-25 planes they were flying out of the base. Planes would come down low over Tuck'em Inn and fire their fifty-caliber machine guns at white targets erected on the beach.

A special permit was needed to go on the water, and this approval was issued by the Captain of the Port of Georgetown who was Lieutenant Don Richardson of Bucksport. Permits, like a driver's license, had your picture and description on them and were stamped either commercial or pleasure.

One afternoon, thinking the target practice was over, we decided to take a sail in our snipe. As soon as we reached Whale Creek, a squadron of B-25s came over and began shooting at our sails which they mistook for targets. We all got out and dove under the boat, letting down the sails as quickly as possible and remaining under the water until the firing stopped. It was a harrowing experience, one which we did not repeat.

I signed up for the Coast Guard Reserve and operated ten days a month patrolling North Inlet, Winyah Bay, and North and South Santee bays in my boat *Suzanne*. We reported to the Captain of the Port of Georgetown before departure to pick up our assignment and supplies like flares, side arms, and a Thompson gun. Our job was to see that no boats came in or out of the inlets or bays without proper permits and recognition signals, and if there were any infractions of the rules, we were to take the culprits back to Georgetown for discipline.

This was pleasant work but tedious, and we had to take turns on watch day and night. If it was duck season, we would take shotguns and pull a small boat, taking advantage of our location for some good shooting. We would also fish in season, and, at first, I could choose my own crew, usually Julian Rogers, Bill Hall, William Hubbard, Baker McIntyre, or sometimes Luther Byars or McKoy Rose.

We had some rough weather and funny experiences. Once we were anchored in North Inlet between Debordieu Beach and North Island and saw some blinking lights in the creek behind Debordieu. Because any lights on the water were strictly prohibited, we had to up anchor and investigate. Upon locating the culprits, we found two old men seining for fish. They had a lantern in a bucket, and when they pulled out the lantern to see their catch, it looked as if they were signaling. They were surprised to see us, but because they had no permits, we had to take them to Georgetown for trial.

One trip John Blackwell, a Marion merchant, asked if we would take three of his homing pigeons with us and release them about a hundred miles from Marion so he could check their speed in returning home. The pigeons were released from their cage near Murphy Island on the North Santee Bay on Friday morning at the agreed upon time. We watched as they circled overhead and headed home. One of them lit in a dead tree, but the others flew on. When I reached Marion on Monday, I called John to ask about the pigeons, only one of which had returned. He told me later that the second one did not return for a week, and the third never showed. Pigeons, like the rest of us, enjoy the coastal breeze and good food.

The Suzanne *goes to war.*

On another patrol, I was given orders by the Captain of the Port to stop Admiral James' barge, which was on the way to Georgetown from Charleston, and to give him new docking instructions. I was told that I would probably meet the barge between South Island and the entrance to the Sampit River. They did not tell me *how* to stop the ship, only to stop it. On board we discussed how to do the job with no signal flags. We decided to turn the yachting ensign upside down and wave it as if we were in distress. On meeting the barge on lower Winyah Bay, Julian Rogers stood at the bow and waved the flag. They did stop. I climbed aboard to deliver the message, forgetting the customary salute to the flag and officer of the deck, but the admiral thanked us for the message and complimented our reserve forces for their work.

On one trip McKoy Rose was with us. He hit the icy deck early one morning, slipped, and did a perfect half gainer into the water. We fished him out, but he had lost his teeth and his glasses. We spent several hours trying to find them with no luck.

Patroling in North Santee Bay during duck season, we were carrying guns, a small boat, and decoys. We left the *Suzanne* early in the morning to get out on a small island and place the decoys. All set for some good shooting, we were surprised by a caretaker in a small boat who wanted to arrest us for trespassing on the property of the Santee Gun Club, a group of wealthy New Yorkers who hunted there in season. Arguing for quite a while to no avail, I finally asked the caretaker to show us his federal permit to be on the water. Of course, he didn't have one and was embarrassed to be breaking federal law and subject to fine and parole by the Captain of the Port. He changed his attitude, gave us several ducks he had shot, and invited us to hunt on Santee Gun Club property any time.

A related incident occurred on the South Santee River when we were asked to take mail and supplies to a mounted beach patrol on Murphy Island, stationed there to arrest and hold any suspicious characters until some officer arrived to identify them or to take them to the Captain of the Port for questioning.

Murphy Island was owned by the Santee Gun Club. When we reached the island, we found that the coast guard patrol stationed there had rounded up a group of men dressed in hunting clothes who had landed on the island in a small plane. This was about the time that spies were landed on our coast by submarine, and the coast guard boys were sure thay had rounded up English-speaking German spies.

The patrol had followed orders, arrested the men, and kept them under guard for two days without a bath or shave. By the time we arrived, the prisoners were frantic, for they had flown in for a day's duck shooting and were scheduled to be back in New York that same night.

The patrol boys were embarrassed, but everyone understood war measures and realized that coast guard recruits from South Dakota and Nevada might not be expected to know a New York millionaire from a German spy.

The Santee Gun Club has given the island to South Carolina as a game preserve, but they have retained hunting rights and have wished off the taxes and upkeep on the state. The gun club must have had some Philadelphia lawyers as members.

23

CRUISES ON THE SUZANNES II AND III

Presbyterian churches are governed by officers called elders, who meet in regular sessions to oversee the general welfare of the church.

In Marion the elders met monthly; and every other month, the meeting was held in the home or club of one of the group. When my time came to entertain the session, I invited the elders to an all-day meeting and trip down the Waccamaw River on the *Suzanne II*.

Everyone was enthusiastic, and Suzanne prepared a good picnic with some of Catherine Sparkman's fried chicken, potato salad, sandwiches, deviled eggs, pickles, and a slice of cake for dessert.

We met at Bucksport where the boat was docked. Before starting the engine and casting off, our pastor Ben Ormand opened the session meeting with prayer and asked the Clerk of the Session, C.B. Fleetwood, to call the roll and keep the minutes. Then we cruised down the Waccamaw, stopped for gas at Wachesaw, then cruised through Thoroughfare Creek to the Great Pee Dee River and past the beautiful plantations between there and Georgetown. We made a stop at Arundel plantation now owned by Alex Quattlebaum of Florence, who is also a Presbyterian. He had instructed his caretaker to show us through the house and grounds, and we were all impressed with his restoration of the beautiful house and the slave quarters in the rear. After Arundel we passed Chicora Wood, another beautiful rice plantation once owned by Robert F. W. Allston, governor of South Carolina.

We joined the Black River about ten miles above Georgetown, our destination. After tying up on the Sampit River behind the stores, we fired up the galley stove, made coffee, and ate lunch. We left Georgetown about two o'clock and took the Waccamaw route back to Bucksport. Crossing Winyah Bay, we fed the gulls the remains of our lunch. You would be surprised how well they liked pimiento cheese sandwiches. We passed Brookgreen and Sandy Island on the return trip and docked the *Suzanne II* at Bucksport around five o'clock.

Elders who made the trip with me were C.B. Fleetwood, Howard Jones, S.M. Witherspoon, John Seabrook, George Terrell, and Pastor Ormand.

This may be the only session meeting to be held on a boat. It is duly recorded in our church records which are now with the Presbyterian Archives at Montreat, North Carolina. I'm sure the Lord forgave us for not sticking to the agenda on this trip. He was sure to be pleased with our appreciation of his natural wonders which we saw that day.

Another trip Presbyterians enjoyed on the Waccamaw was in 1970 when we invited the young people of the Marion Presbyterian Church for lunch and a cruise from Wachesaw Landing to Georgetown on the *Suzanne III*. Estimating about fifteen young people in the group, we wound up with forty passengers. Freddie Zeman on the *Seven Z's* came to our rescue and we divided the group into four parts. Half went with Freddie and with me from Wachesaw to Georgetown, and the other half met in Georgetown and came back to Wachesaw on the boats.

It was a merry crowd. The ricebirds and redwings hadn't heard so much singing and laughter since the days when everyone in the area traveled by water and the oarsmen sang as they rowed.

On another trip down the Waccamaw on the *Suzanne II* with the late Bill Hall, we saw a large crowd of people at the Mt. Arena Landing on Sandy Island. Slowing the boat to a near stop, we saw a Cadillac hearse with much chrome trim and fancy curtains stop at the landing on the mainland. A minister and undertaker in robes got out, and pallbearers with flowers pinned to their lapels placed a casket on the school boat. After they crossed the river, the pallbearers took the casket from the boat and put it on a flat cart pulled by a yoke of oxen. The pallbearers and guests walked beside the cart and up the hill to the cemetery. The passage demonstrated the link of modern world to the past. Bill and I went ashore for the last of the funeral. When the casket was lowered, each of the pallbearers was given a shovel, and they covered the grave together while the guests chanted one of their favorite spirituals.

On another trip past Sandy Island on a Sunday afternoon in June, we saw a large crowd of people at the Mt. Arena Landing having a baptism in the river. A group dressed in white were standing near the water, and the minister in white robe was waist deep in the river. He supported a teen-aged girl in his arms and carefully lowered her under and

The Suzanne II *with the Presbyterian elders.*

raised her from the water three times. Church members on the shore were swaying, clapping their hands, and chanting "Hallelujah, Hallelujah, Praise the Lord." Isabel and Tom Goodwin from Augusta were with us on this trip, and we all agreed that this was one of the most impressive church services we had ever witnessed.

In the spring of 1975 we invited Edna and Malcolm McLendon and the Harold Bishops to go with us on the *Suzanne III,* from Wachesaw Marina to Georgetown on the Waccamaw River. We took a picnic lunch and had a good run down the river, counting the osprey nests in the trees along the bank and on top of the channel markers and watching the young birds poke their heads above the nests, mouths open and waiting for food brought by their mother or father.

We tied up in Georgetown on the Sampit River and walked along Front Street to the old market which is now the Rice Museum. From there we went to the Prince George Winyah Church which was built before the Revolutionary War. Since we had stopped to read epitaphs on the old tombstones, it was late when we returned to the boat and started back. Heading north on the river with a fair tide and wind, we came out from behind Butler's Island and saw a small boat with an outboard motor attached running in circles. Several of us looked at the boat with the binoculars and thought at first that it was just some boy out on the river to have fun, but we soon realized that the boat was running wild with no one in it.

Sure that someone had fallen overboard, we began circling the river to see if anyone were in the water needing help. I called the coast guard on the radio telephone to report our findings and position, then we stopped by Hagley and asked a fisherman to call the Georgetown Rescue Squad on the shore phone.

We continued to search the river until almost dark, when we gave up and continued our trip to Wachesaw Marina. The dock attendant there had no report of missing persons, and all small boats from the marina had returned safely. After securing our boat, we returned to Marion by car, wondering what had happened.

Several days later the district manager of the B.C. Moore chain of department stores was in my office and told me about a man from Cheraw missing from a fishing trip. At that time no one knew what had happened to him. About a week later, we read in the paper that the Georgetown Rescue Squad had found the body of the Cheraw fisherman in the Intracoastal Waterway and that the body was badly cut and bruised as if it had been hit by a boat propeller.

The story continued to say that two men from Cheraw fishing on the Waccamaw had run out of cigarettes or bait and had stopped at a boat landing to walk to a nearby store. While one was fetching the needed supplies, the other evidently decided to do a little fishing alone and had fallen from the boat after it was underway.

On another cruise when I owned Beet Island near Beaufort, South Carolina, I decided to combine business and pleasure. I asked Harold Bishop, a Marion forester, to come along to cruise the timber growing on the island and determine the best location for planting additional trees. I invited Bubba Clemmons and Bob McCollum for their good company. Each had a task on the boat when we were docking or getting under way: Bubba and Harold were to handle the bow and stern lines, and Bob was to be sure the tow line of the dink did not get caught in the propeller.

We left from Bucksport, had a good run to Charleston, tied up for the night at the Municipal Yacht Basin, and walked over to Everett's to try some of their famous she-crab soup and other seafood for supper. Next morning we were awake early and decided to cook breakfast underway. Just as we were leaving the dock, the engine coughed, spit, then stopped. The dink's towline had wound around the shaft and choked the motor.

I do not know whether Bob had had too much she-crab soup the night before or was looking at a pretty girl on a nearby yacht, but he had neglected his duty. I had to get in the cold water and cut the rope from the propeller and shaft.

The rest of the trip was uneventful, but Bob was in the doghouse. Harold cruised the timber on the island and made his recommendations. Bubba tried to catch a marsh coon without luck. We returned home by Charleston and again ate at Everett's, but no she-crab soup for Bob.

24

EBB TIDE

The tide is going out on Rum Gully Swash. The oystercatchers are standing on their favorite rocks waiting for the oysters to open so they can have their daily feast.

The marsh is turning brown and the harvest moon is on the wane. Oyster-roast signs are appearing in front of the eating places on Highway 17. Gurdon Tarbox has his gardeners planting winter grass on the roadside near the entrance to Brookgreen. The ducks and geese in V-formations are flying south.

Bill Carmichael is cleaning his decoys for the approaching duck season, and Tommy Chandler is feeding his Labrador retriever special food.

Mary Walker is covering her collards in the vegetable garden to keep them from freezing. Clarke Willcox has his handyman out cutting wood for the fireplace, and Genevieve Peterkin is in her back yard raking and burning leaves.

The sailboat has been rolled into the boathouse. Tuck'em Inn is being readied for the winter. The rocking chairs are pushed back against the wall, and the hammocks are folded and put under the beds. It is the close of another good summer at Tuck'em Inn, and the old house is being shut for the winter for the seventy-sixth time.

The crabs are burrowing under the sand or mud to keep warm—going to bed and pulling up the blanket, the old timers call it. The sand fiddlers are waving their big claws in farewell. The writer is approaching his eighty-first year. It has been a good summer with good companions and good stories. Good-bye.

Gone But Not Forgotten
Here Lies
Tuck 'em Inn
Born
June 12, 1914
Died
September 21, 1989
Hurricane Hugo & Company
Undertakers
She Will Rise Again

B.P.G.